Pass the Port *Again*

The best after-dinner stories of the famous

Pass the Port *Again*

The best after-dinner stories of the famous

Christian Brann
Cirencester

ISBN 0 9504923 3 7

© Christian Brann Limited 1980

Published to advance the work of

The stories in this book
were generously donated
by their famous contributors
to Oxfam, to whom all
royalties will be given.

First published 1980
Revised edition 1981
Second revised edition October 1981

This book was devised, published and printed by
Christian Brann Limited, Cirencester, Glos.
Illustrations by Brian Blake

Introduction

The work of OXFAM is supported by thousands of organisations and individual supporters in many ways, ranging from single donations to large legacies. All of these are used to help those in need all over the world.

Four years ago Christian Brann came to us with the idea of publishing a book containing the best after-dinner stories of famous people.

His company offered to take responsibility for all the work of collecting contributions, editing them, printing the books and distributing them. OXFAM was promised all the royalties and the revenue from copies bought direct by supporters.

Since then, almost 100,000 copies of PASS THE PORT have been sold and OXFAM has benefited to the tune of almost £50,000. Even now, every week, orders come in for copies of the hardbound and softbound editions. It was, therefore, decided to publish a second volume and here it is: PASS THE PORT *AGAIN*: nearly 500 additional stories, some from authors who contributed to the first volume and others from new ones.

We all wish to express our gratitude to our distinguished contributors and to Christian Brann: we hope that you will enjoy this book as much as you enjoyed Volume I. At the same time you will have the satisfaction of knowing that you have helped the work of OXFAM in relieving distress all over the world.

Brian W. Walker
Director
Oxfam
274 Banbury Road
Oxford

Autumn 1980

Sir George Abell, K.C.I.E., O.B.E.,
Formerly Indian Civil Service.

Told by Archbishop Fisher at the Guildhall Banquet in November 1957.
I heard a schoolboy, in answer to a question on heredity, say:
"Well, sir, heredity is like this. If your grandfather had no children and
your father had no children, you would be likely to have no children too."

Sir Godfrey Agnew, K.C.V.O., C.B.,
Clerk of the Privy Council, 1953–74.

It is seldom the coldest girl who gets the mink coat.

Doctor to patient: "There is a 50/50 chance
of success in this operation. You will be O.K."
Patient: "Why will I be O.K.?"
Doctor: "The first 50 have already died."

Major-General John B. Akehurst, C.B.E.,
Commanding 4th Armoured Division, British Army of the Rhine.

Invited to speak at the annual dinner of the Anglo/Omani Society, I
dipped into *Pass the Port* for some suitable humour. I found nothing ideal
under 'Middle East' or related subjects, but discovered an ideal opening
story contributed by The Hon. Ivor Lucas, who I knew to be a leading light
at the Foreign Office Middle East desk. The story was a happy little joke
about ancient Rome and after-dinner speaking.

Driving to the dinner I was held up by a massive traffic jam, in which I
sat worrying about the time and mentally rehearsing my speech. Eventually I arrived only two minutes before everyone went in to dinner; just in
time, in fact, to be introduced to the other guest speaker (who was to speak
first) — The Hon. Ivor Lucas!

When a senior officer visits a unit there is a tendency, as he goes among the soldiers, for too many of the questions and the answers to be the same.

Confronted by a line of a dozen soldiers, and trying to ask each a different question, I enquired of one whether he were married.

"Just, sir," came the reply, so naturally I offered my warmest congratulations and followed up by asking when the happy day had been.

"When I say 'Just,' sir, I mean '*Just*,' sir," came the reply. "I am only just married, and my divorce comes through next week!"

Three men awaited execution by firing squad in the condemned cell, from which the site of their forthcoming ordeal could be clearly seen.

The first, an Englishman, was taken out and stood against the wall. As the firing squad raised their rifles, he suddenly shouted "Avalanche!" at the top of his voice. The soldiers looked about in alarm, threw down their rifles and turned to run. Taking advantage of the momentary chaos, the Englishman scampered away as fast as his legs would carry him and escaped.

The second condemned man, a Scot, seeing the success of this ploy, when his turn came shouted "Flood!", with exactly the same highly successful effect, and off he ran.

The third man, an Irishman, impressed by the initiative of his colleagues, determined to follow suit. As the rifles were raised and fingers curled around the triggers, he shouted "Fire!".

Earl Alexander of Tunis.

On occasions I have felt rather like the parson who had been transferred to a new parish and hadn't prepared a sermon. Mounting the pulpit, he said the following:

"Dearly beloved brethren, I must confess that due to other pressures I haven't had time to prepare a sermon, so I shall just have to repeat the words that God puts into my mouth. However, next week I shall prepare a much better sermon."

Lord Allen of Abbeydale, G.C.B.,
Member, Crown Agents' Tribunal.

It was a beautiful evening, and the ruins of the ancient temple, redolent with age, looked most impressive lit up by the setting sun.

The tourists gazed at them in awe.

"How old are the ruins?" one of them ventured to ask the local guide.

"4,007 years," came the prompt reply.

"But how can you be sure of the precise year?" asked the tourist.

"Oh," said the guide, "the leader of the team who excavated the ruins told us that they were 4,000 years old — and that was seven years ago."

The somewhat disgruntled young American sat down to yet another meal at the small French inn.

He picked up the menu and with sinking heart read the opening words 'Soupe du jour'.

"What," he said, "again?".

Professor George Allen, C.B.E., F.B.A.,
Emeritus Professor of Political Economy, University College, London.

Soon after Goethe had died, honoured by the whole of the civilised world, a biographer, in search of information about the great man's youth, visited the village in Alsace which had been the scene of Goethe's early love affair with Frederika.

His enquiries brought him to the house of an old lady who well remembered both the lovers.

"Yes," she said, "Goethe was a fine young man and Frederika a charming girl. They saw much of one another, and everyone here expected them to make a match of it. But, one day, Goethe suddenly packed his bags and made off. *And, from that time to this, no one has ever heard anything more about him.*"

Rear-Admiral Courtney Anderson, C.B., Editor, Admiralty 'Board Bulletin', 1971–78.

Brevity and clarity are vital to good staff work. The Naval Staff Course teaches this with the story of 'Pug' Ismay who waded through a long waffling, nonsensical paper and summed it up by writing tersely at the bottom one short word.

Then realising it had to go to the Prime Minister, he lost his nerve and, feeling that although his sentiment was admirable his wording lacked finesse, he scratched out the word and substituted 'Round objects'.

In so doing he doubled the length of his minute and sacrificed his clarity, for the paper came back from Mr. Churchill with the query:

"Pray, who is Mr. Round and why does he object?"

Brigadier David W. Anderson, C.B.E., Formerly Infantry Brigade Commander, Northern Ireland.

Visiting general to Scots corporal who is just back from a patrol near Crossmaglen:

"And how many tours have you had in Ulster, Corporal?"

Corporal: "About five or six, sir."

General: "When were you last here, Corporal?"

Corporal: "About two years ago, sir."

General (beginning to wonder how to keep this conversation going): "And what has changed in the last two years, Corporal?"

Corporal (after pausing, looks general straight in the eye and says): "I'm two years older, sir!"

The Marquess of Anglesey,
Military Historian; Chairman, Historic Buildings Council for Wales.

In 1820, my great-great-grandfather, the first Marquess of Anglesey, who had lost his leg at the battle of Waterloo, supported the Bill of 'Pains and Penalties' against Queen Caroline, by which George IV, newly come to the throne, hoped to divorce his wife on the ground of her misconduct and adultery.

The hostility of the pro-Caroline mob had no effect upon Anglesey. On one occasion he is said to have been surrounded in the street by an angry crowd who barred his progress till he should give 'The Queen!'. Complying, he said, "God save the Queen — and may all your wives be like her!" (Whatever the sins of the King, the profligacy of the Queen was at least as bad!)

Sir John Arbuthnot, Bt., M.B.E., T.D.,
Erstwhile M.P. for Dover; Church Commissioner.

Stalin, Truman and Churchill were all promised that one wish would be granted. Stalin asked for the annihilation of the U.S.A. Truman asked for the complete subjugation of the U.S.S.R. Churchill said:

"I would like a whishky and shoda, but I am in no hurry, pray serve the other gentlemen first."

Husband on a business trip abroad sent his wife a telegram:
"Having a wonderful time, wish you were here." In transmission the final 'e' was left out.

The Rt. Hon. Peter Archer, Q.C., M.P.,
Formerly Solicitor General.

Lawyers and judges have something in common with chimpanzees. The higher they climb, the more they display their less attractive features.

Professor Bernard Ashmole, C.B.E., M.C.,
Lecturer on Greek and Roman Art.

I was discussing with a Swedish colleague the various disasters that can befall a lantern lecturer on tour in the United States (or elsewhere for that matter). For example, the room is in bright sunlight and there are no blinds; there is no reading desk, or a desk but no reading light; the slides won't fit the lantern or they won't focus; the lantern fuses or bursts into flames — and so on.

He then said: "Oh! but something happened to me which must be far worse than anything that can have happened to you. It was in a brand new fully automated lecture hall in California, and when I went to look at it the morning before my lecture, my sponsor showed me how beautifully it was fitted out. There was a splendid desk for the lecturer, with a row of buttons on each side. 'This one,' he said, 'closes the window-blinds, this one dims the light, this one extinguishes the lights, this one changes your slides, and this revolving one works your electric pointer. You needn't worry about the others; they don't really concern you.'

"When I came to lecture, everything went well: after I had made my opening remarks I blacked out the room successfully, and the first slide and following ones duly appeared when I pressed the button. After a while I became so absorbed in my subject that I leaned forward and rested my elbows on the desk, and unfortunately also on both rows of buttons. There was a powerful grinding noise, and the audience slowly sank out of sight: simultaneously the sections of a dance floor closed in over their heads, and in just about a minute I found myself alone in an empty ballroom."

"What did you do?" I asked.

"What could I do?" he answered. "I went home."

Before the days of good lantern-slides the elderly Professor of Anatomy at University College, London, used at a certain moment of the lecture to tell the lab. boy to uncover a specimen consisting of a frog, beautifully dissected and displayed. One day, however, when the cover was taken off, instead of the frog there appeared two hardboiled eggs and a sandwich.

"That's strange," said the professor; "and I'm sure I ate my lunch!"

**Sir George Astbury, J.P.,
Hon. Alderman for Cheshire.**

The South Staffordshire narrow canal boatman's horse was taken ill and sadly died. He bought another, slightly bigger, horse and unfortunately when passing under a low bridge the horse became stuck. He went to his boat and got a hammer and chisel and proceeded to chip away at the brickwork.

Presently a policeman appeared on the bridge and, looking down, asked him what he was doing. The boatee replied:

"Cor yo see? Me hoss is stuck."

The policeman suggested that the boatee should get a shovel and dig underneath the horse's feet. The boatee looked up at the policeman and said with such scorn and derision:

"You'll never get promotion. Cor yo see? It's his ruddy yed what's stuck, not his ruddy feet!"

**Sir Alec Atkinson, K.C.B., D.F.C.,
Second Permanent Secretary, Department of Health and Social Security,
1977–79.**

A centipede began suffering cruelly from rheumatism and went to consult the wise owl.

"I suppose that it is most troublesome in the winter?" asked the owl.

"Yes," replied the centipede.

"In that case I would recommend that you become a dormouse and lie up snug the winter through."

The centipede was turning away, delighted, when doubt spread over his tiny features.

"But how do I become a dormouse?" he asked.

"Don't bother me with details," the owl replied, "I am a policy making owl."

On an ecumenical occasion, a Non-conformist minister expressed, to a Roman Catholic priest, his keen pleasure that they should be sharing the same platform. The priest said that he also was pleased. Then he added:

"After all, we both worship the same God. You in your way, and I in God's way."

Lord Balfour of Inchrye, P.C., M.C.,
Parliamentary Under-Secretary of State for Air, 1938-44.

One evening, Mr. Churchill, as he then was, was in the Smoking Room of the House of Commons when shown an article in the evening paper on the Mount Everest conquest. Asked what he thought of the great achievement, his comment was:

"I do not wish to overrate chastity, but there is much to be said for virgin mountains."

Sir John Balfour, G.C.M.G., G.B.E.,
Retired British Ambassador.

Early in 1937 I went to Oxford, as a pre-1914 member of the Raleigh Club, to attend a dinner at which Winston Churchill was a guest of honour. In his speech on this occasion he said:

"People say that the Nazi-Fascists and Communists are poles apart. So they are, but if you went to the North or the South Poles what would you find? A few more penguins here, a few less polar bears there—but in either place the same bleak, desolate landscape swept by the bitter winds of death."

Lieut.-Colonel Sir Donald Bannerman, Bt.,
Formerly Senior Control Officer, Military Government, Germany.

A young barrister was speaking on behalf of his client, an old lady, who had been knocked down by a car and fractured her jaw.

"And now," he concluded, "my client is no longer able to bite her bottom with her upper teeth."

Sir Roderick Barclay, G.C.V.O., K.C.M.G.,
Formerly British Ambassador to Denmark and Belgium.

When Ernie Bevin was Foreign Secretary, I took him a brace of pheasants as a present one day and offered to give them to his driver to take back to his flat.

He replied: "You give them to me, my boy. I'm not too grand to carry me dinner 'ome."

Sir Richard Barlas, K.C.B., O.B.E.,
Clerk of the House of Commons.

I learnt early in the 'thirties that military orders should always be taken with a grain of salt — a lesson that was to prove invaluable early in the 'forties.

When I was up at Oxford I joined the University Cavalry Squadron, more with a view to free riding than in any expectation of glory. On the death of his late Majesty King George V, the Squadron was honoured to be ordered to line the streets on the approach to St. George's Chapel at Windsor on the occasion of the State Funeral.

On arrival at Windsor we were told that we would be lining the right-hand side of the street leading up to the Chapel and should be marched there in single file. The correct words of command for dismounted cavalry to get into single file were something that neither the Squadron Commander (an undergraduate from New College) nor the Squadron knew much about; however, this was achieved in the light of notice and we were duly marched off. On arriving at our position we were correctly halted. The Squadron Commander should then have given the command, "Left turn" so that the Squadron had their backs to the crowd and would face the cortège when it arrived. Unfortunately he said, "Right turn".

Those of the Squadron who were later to become Staff Officers knew the importance of obeying orders to the letter, and turned right to face the crowd. Those of us who took a more relaxed view of military discipline followed the spirit rather than the letter of the order and turned as we thought the Squadron Commander would have wished us to, if he had been on top of his form. Half the Squadron was thus turned one way, the other half the other way.

But worse was to come. Instead of giving the order, "As you were", our unfortunate Commander told us to "About turn". While this was, of course, simple for the prospective Staff Officers who were now facing the correct way, it left the remainder in a terrible quandary and most, though not all, did "About turn", so the Squadron was no better off!

After that there was only one thing to do and the Squadron C.O. did it. On the command, "Carry on, Sarn't Major", a grizzled veteran of Omdurman, shouted at the Squadron, "Get stuck in with your backs to the crowd"; this may not have come out of the drill book, but it was clear and unequivocal. Order was restored.

General Sir Hugh Beach, G.B.E., K.C.B., M.C.,
Master-General of the Ordnance.

A young wife had just seen her husband off to work and went upstairs to take a bath. As she was putting her foot in the water she remembered that the gas stove was still burning in the kitchen and should not have been. There was no one else in the house so, without putting on her bath wrap she went down to turn the gas off. As she was doing so she heard footsteps coming to the back door.

Now the arrangement was that the milkman brought the milk bottles right into the kitchen to prevent the tits from drinking the cream. So she dashed for the nearest door, which was the cupboard where they kept brooms and things. Just in time.

The back door opened and the footsteps came into the kitchen. But then to her horror they came on across the kitchen and the cupboard door was flung open. It was the gas man come to read the meter. It was difficult to think what to say. What she did say was:

"I'm so sorry, I was expecting the milkman."

Sir Terence Beckett, C.B.E.,
Director-General, C.B.I.

A businessman walking across Westminster Bridge was shocked to see another businessman on the parapet about to jump. He asked: "Why?" The second man began to explain — the government, the trade unions, difficult customers...

"Oh, come down and tell me all about it," said the first man, "it can't be as bad as all that."

Five minutes later they were both standing on the parapet.

**Sir Adrian Beecham, Bt.,
Musical Composer.**

My favourite story about my illustrious progenitor, Sir Thomas Beecham, the authenticity for which I can vouch, having heard it from his own lips, is as follows.

Being about to rehearse an orchestra during a concert tour in Sicily, my father was warned that he should be cautious in his handling of one of the wind players who was reputed to be a member of a local society which had the power of life and death. As the rehearsal progressed, divers unmusical sounds issued from this gentleman's instrument. My father exercised unusual restraint, until a beautiful *andante sostenuto* passage was marred by an unauthorised fanfare from the gentleman in question. Unable to contain himself any longer, my father cried:

"For God's sake, kill me at once and have done with it!"

In my early youth, I was having lessons in composition from Dr. Allen, afterwards Sir Hugh Allen, at Oxford. The poem I was setting to music for him contained, like so many other poems, the word 'love'.

Whilst discussing the composition with him, I said:

"Don't you think that we should have sweet harmony on this word?" At which he burst out:

"Why? Why? Why should you? You know *nothing* about it! Absolutely nothing! Let us have a r-r-rasping discord!"

I might have been more impressed by this piece of advice had I not heard rumours of his matrimonial infelicity.

**Professor Alfred Beeston, F.B.A.,
Emeritus Professor of Arabic, Oxford.**

At the end of the American Civil War, a town just north of the north-south border decided to celebrate the peace by a banquet to which representatives of the south were invited. One of these was a southern colonel, who was asked by his friends after he got back what it had been like.

"Well," he said, "they were very hospitable; but I found myself sitting next to a Negro, a thing I have never done in my life."

"Why, Colonel," they said, "that must have been dreadful; however did you address him?" His answer was:

"Well, that was a problem. I could not bring myself to call him 'Sir', as I would with a gentleman, and in view of the occasion, I did not like to call him 'damn nigger' as I would ordinarily have done, so I compromised; I called him 'Professor'."

**Air Chief Marshal Sir Michael Beetham, G.C.B., C.B.E., D.F.C., A.F.C., A.D.C.,
Chief of the Air Staff.**

Let me tell you the story of a keen golfer who had been arrested for killing his wife. When the trial came he was overcome with remorse and when the judge asked him:

"How did you kill her?"

"With three strokes of a No. 9 iron!" he replied.

"Three strokes?" queried the judge.

"Yes, your Lordship," he said. "On the first two I lifted my head!"

**Hon. Sir George Bellew, K.C.B., K.C.V.O.,
Formerly Garter Principal King of Arms.**

Col. Murgatroyd: "Now tell me, old friend — what do you think of my new wife?"

Capt. Carruthers: "Well, sir, if I may venture, as an old family friend, to speak freely — I don't like her."

Col. Murgatroyd: "No? Nor do I. Pass the port."

Sir Robert Bellinger, G.B.E.,
Former Lord Mayor of London.

A traveller in Ireland
arrived at a railway station
to leave on a 9 a.m. train.
Noticing the clock outside
the station recording
8.55 a.m., he entered a
newspaper shop to purchase some
reading material.

Upon entering the station platform
he arrived just in time to see the
9 a.m. train departing, with a clock
above the platform indicating
9.05 a.m. (just 5 minutes ahead of the clock outside the station).

After protesting to the Station Master that he had lost his train owing to
the clocks not being synchronised, he was admonished with the retort:

"And what would we be needing two clocks for, if they both told the
same time?"

Sir Max Beloff,
Historian; Fellow, St. Antony's College, Oxford.

There is a story of which the late Sir Lewis Namier was very fond. A
country priest in old Russia wanted to explain to a peasant the meaning of
the word 'miracle'.

"Suppose," he said, "I were to climb to the top of the church steeple and
jump down and arrive unharmed on the ground. What would you call
that?"

"Luck," said the peasant.

"Well, suppose I jumped again," said the priest, "and landed safely once
more, what would you say then?"

"Luck again," said the peasant.

"But suppose I did it yet a third time and escaped unscathed, what would
you say?"

"Habit," said the peasant.

Sir Max Bemrose,
Ex-High Sheriff, Derbyshire; Chairman, National Union Conservative and
Unionist Associations, 1964–65.

We have a maiden aunt in our family and the legend is that some years ago she decided after forty years of city life to retire and start a poultry farm.

She bought a house in the country with some land and huts close by. Then she went off to acquire her stock of poultry. She came back quite pleased with herself, having ordered sixty hens and sixty cocks.

Sir John Benn, Bt.,
Formerly Chairman, several British and American companies.

Late one evening the lift in a large city office carried its eleven occupants down six floors non-stop to the basement. They had to be rescued through a trap door in the roof of the lift car, which was clearly labelled to hold 'Not more than six passengers'.

When the secretary of the company reported this incident to the Board, he said:

"What worries me, gentlemen, is that the culprits were our auditors, who evidently can neither read nor count."

An employer was upbraiding George for being constantly late for work.

"How is it that you, who live almost next door to the factory, are so often late, whereas Charlie, who lives a mile away, is always on time?"

"It's like this, sir," was the reply. "If Charlie is late he can run and catch up but if I'm late I'm 'ere."

Admiral Sir Peter Berger, K.C.B., M.V.O., D.S.C.,
Flag Officer Plymouth.

During my very earliest days as a cadet in the navy, just about the first thing which our seamanship instructor — an old gnarled Chief Petty Officer called Searle — attempted to teach us, was how to tie an obscure and complicated knot (or was it a bend or a hitch?) called a Double Matthew

Walker. This proved to be completely beyond my ham-fisted capabilities and so one morning, with the impetuous folly of youth, I had the peevish temerity to ask Chief Petty Officer Searle what on earth a Double Matthew Walker was used for anyway.

He paused for but the fraction of a second, before transfixing me with a beady eye and sternly replying:

"That knot, young man, is used for special purposes, when and as required."

Sir Isaiah Berlin, O.M., C.B.E.,
Fellow of All Souls College, Oxford.

Lord Chief Justice Hewart once when receiving some kind of public honour said, in reply:

"On occasions of this kind there are two speeches which I can make; one is short and one is long. The short one is 'Thank you', the long one is 'Thank you very much'. Now that I have acquainted you with the content of both speeches I see no reason for making either."

Sir Kenneth Berrill, K.C.B.,
Head of the Government's 'Think Tank'.

A friend was, years ago, being interviewed for the headship of a Church of England prep. school. He was not all that keen on getting the job and the interviewing governors were formal and stuffy. Eventually one asked:

"Tell me, if you did become headmaster, what would be your main aim in educating those boys?"

Friend (tongue in cheek): "My aim, sir, would be to turn them into Christian gentlemen."

Governor (testily): "Yes, yes, but what exactly does that mean?"

Friend: "With which of the terms are you unfamiliar?"

Major-General Donald A.D.J. Bethell,
Formerly Commanding the Chestnut Troop, R.H.A.

The doting father asked his small daughter what she would like for Christmas. Shyly she announced that she would like a baby brother. To everyone's surprise and delight her mother returned from hospital on Christmas Eve with the baby boy in her arms.

Father repeated the question next year. There was less hesitation.

"If it wouldn't be too uncomfortable for mummy, I'd like a pony."

Nicholas Bethell,
Writer and Translator; Member of European Parliament (London North-West).

The judge addressed the prisoner in the dock sternly:

"Seamus O'Reilly, you are charged with the crime of theft. How do you plead? Are you guilty or not guilty?"

O'Reilly: "I don't know, my Lord. I haven't heard the evidence yet."

The Late Professor Stanley Thomas Bindoff,
Professor of History, Queen Mary College, University of London, 1951–75.

Early in the last war I took over a course of lectures from a colleague who had been called up for military service. When several weeks later he returned on leave before being posted abroad he offered to resume the lectures temporarily and I agreed. Unfortunately I neglected to tell him which part of the syllabus I had dealt with in his absence and he therefore began his first lecture by saying:

"I don't know what Mr. Bindoff has been talking about in his lectures!"

A voice from the back of the class replied:

"Nor do we."

The Hon. Lord Birsay, K.T., C.B.E., T.D.,
Ex-Chairman, Scottish Land Court.

I was extolling my longevity. Richness of experience from the horse-drawn cart to Concorde. Said a friend:
"You make yourself as old as Methuselah."
"Yes," said I, "I was with Moses when he got the tablets."
"I ken that," came the reply, "I gie'd ye them!"

Professor Richard Bishop, C.B.E.,
Kennedy Professor of Mechanical Engineering, University College London.

Soon after the war I went to Stanford University in California, and was invited to give a lecture on my home country to some schoolchildren in Redwood City High School. It turned out to be quite an experience, for the kids were absolutely formidable. The thing that I remember most vividly was the teacher's opening of the proceedings:
"The speaker today is Mr. Bishop, who is from England. England is a small island in the Atlantic Ocean. (Remember? That's the one on the right-hand side.) England was in the war and most thinking people now regard England as 'all washed up'. I want you to welcome Mr. Bishop."

Lord Blease, J.P.,
Formerly Northern Ireland Officer, Irish Congress of Trade Unions.

The devil was continually challenging St. Peter to a game of soccer, but St. Peter refused, until one day while walking around heaven he discovered that quite a number of Irish International footballers had entered the 'pearly gates'.
"Now I'll arrange to play you that soccer game." said St. Peter. "How about it?"
"You'll lose," said the devil, "you'll lose."
"Oh, don't be sure," replied St. Peter. "We now have in heaven a great number of International soccer stars from which to select a winning team."
"You'll lose, you'll lose!" repeated the devil.
"What makes you so sure we'll lose?" enquired St. Peter.
"Because," laughed the devil, "we have all the referees down here."

Major-General Peter Blunt, C.B., M.B.E., G.M. (Retired),
Managing Director London companies.

An elderly man was beaten badly by thugs and left lying in the gutter, bleeding and in great pain. The first passer-by averted his gaze; the second likewise. Nobody wanted to know until a social worker on her way home passed by. She looked down at the recumbent figure and said:

"Tut, tut, whoever did this needs help."

Sir Frederic Bolton, M.C.,
Shipowner; President, General Council of British Shipping, 1975–76.

He had ordered a very large tanker at the height of the boom, and was forced to take delivery, on credit, at the bottom of the slump.

He had no cargoes for her, and his bankers would support him no longer and, as a last resort, he wandered into a church where he was shortly joined by a beggar, loud in his entreaties to the Almighty for relief from his difficulties.

The shipowner stood it for a while, and then slid along the pew to the other and pressed £25, to the beggar's delight, into his hand. As the beggar went on his way rejoicing, the shipowner fell on his knees, saying:

"Now, Lord, if I can have your undivided attention…"

The small girl was allowed to stay up for the start of her parents' dinner party, and as a treat was told she could say Grace. She became tongue-tied and didn't know what to say. Her mother said:

"Say what daddy said before breakfast this morning — you know, 'Oh, God…'," to which the little girl happily responded:

"Oh, God, why have we got to have these terrible people to dinner tonight?"

A hospital visitor stopped to enquire in a kindly fashion about a patient surrounded by pipes coming in and out of him everywhere. As soon as he reached the bedside, the patient showed signs of great distress, grabbed a pencil and paper, scribbled a note, thrust it at the visitor — and fell back dead.

The appalled visitor was hustled out of the hospital in the ensuing confusion and only remembered the note when he was well away from it. He found it was incomprehensively in Chinese. After some effort and some time he found someone who had a friend who could translate. It was returned to him, reading: "Please get off my oxygen pipe!"

**Sir Robert Booth, C.B.E., T.D.,
Chairman, National Exhibition Centre.**

It was one of those late night flights and soon after take-off I was about to settle down when the stewardess appeared. She was exceedingly good-looking and wearing a uniform which was so tight I could hardly breathe.

Maybe it was the champagne, but I suddenly heard myself speaking aloud the subconscious thought:

"Where have you been all my life?"

The beautiful creature must have heard, for she paused, smiled and said:

"Well, I don't really know, sir, but I guess that for about two-thirds of it, I hadn't even been born."

**Major-General Esmond J. Bowen, Q.H.D.S.,
Director, Army Dental Service.**

A good many years ago, in the early days of the Malayan emergency, I was running a pretty hectic 'sick parade' in an Army Dental Centre in Kuala Lumpur. Patients were being seen in quick time and being relieved of their toothache; tooth as well, where appropriate. As one case left the chair I would turn away to wash my hands, at the same time calling in the next.

"Next case, please," I called and, glancing over my shoulder, saw a ginger-haired soldier wearing jungle green uniform and hat come in.

"Sit down, please," said I, washing my hands.

"Shall I take it off, sir?" said the soldier.

"Yes," I replied, knowing how impossible it is for a dentist to treat a patient who is wearing a hat. Drying my hands I turned round. To my utter consternation an absolutely bald-headed soldier was solemnly sitting in the chair. In his lap he held a jungle hat — and a very ginger wig.

Lord Boyd-Carpenter, P.C., D.L.,
Chairman, Rugby Portland Cement Co. Ltd.

A quotation from a County Council circular:
"In the event of a major nuclear attack the County Libraries will be manned only by a skeleton staff."

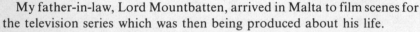

Lord Brabourne,
Film Producer.

My father-in-law, Lord Mountbatten, arrived in Malta to film scenes for the television series which was then being produced about his life.

A reporter from the local radio station met him at the airport and said:

"Lord Mountbatten, I understand that you have come to Malta in connection with a television series entitled, 'The Life and Times of Lord Mountbatten'."

My father-in-law replied that this was the case.

The reporter then said:

"May I ask, Lord Mountbatten, what part will you be playing in this film?"

My father-in-law was enormously amused by this question but was even more astonished when later that evening he heard the interview broadcast without this remarkable question being deleted.

Professor Raymond L. Brett,
G.F. Grant Professor of English, Hull University.

The University Grants Committee is composed of senior and distinguished academics and at the time of this story its chairman was Lord

Wolfenden, who had been Vice-Chancellor of Reading University and who later was to become Director of the British Museum. The Committee pays visits to all universities in turn to assess their financial needs and to discuss their proposals. On this occasion they were on their way to Hull University in a mini-bus which had been provided for them in Leeds.

It was a hot afternoon and as it wore on Lord Wolfenden thought it would be a good idea to stop for a cup of tea. So he directed the driver to pull in at a wayside café and when the bus stopped, jumped down and approached the café in his shirt-sleeves. Before he reached it, however, the door was thrown open and an angry, gesticulating proprietor rushed out. Pointing at a sign on the forecourt, which no one had noticed, he shouted:

"It says 'No Coach Parties' — can't any of you lot read?"

The Marquis of Bristol, G.O.St.A., G.C.L.J.,
Chancellor of the Monarchist League.

My attractive P.A. was heard saying to her assistant (referring to her immediate superior, not myself!):

"Does your boss walk around the room when he is dictating a letter to you?"

Answer (heard by several — many giggles): "Of course not, I would fall off his lap if he did."

Brigadier George V. Britten, C.B.E.,
Former Regular Officer and Member of the Diplomatic Service.

"Did you know that eight men out of ten use a ballpoint pen to write with?" was the title of a poster advertising a talk on modern life to a Women's Club. Beside it someone had written: "No, but what on earth do the other two use a ballpoint pen for?"

Years ago there were gypsies in a field near our church. They suddenly left, leaving a dead donkey behind. Our vicar telephoned the local Council about it and the official who answered, with a sense of humour, said:
"I always understood that it was the duty of a vicar to bury the dead."
"That may be so," replied the vicar, "but I thought I should at least notify the relatives of the deceased."

When we lived in France we found one restaurant listing that well known vodka and tomato juice pick-me-up as 'Bloody Merry'.

Lieut.-Colonel Sir Walter Bromley-Davenport, T.D., D.L.,
Late Grenadier Guards; Conservative M.P., 1945–70.

Y've asked me to write something original,
Some brain wave from within.
But I've nothing original in me
Excepting original sin.

Lord Brown, P.C., M.B.E.,
Minister of State, Board of Trade, 1965–70.

Duncan McPhee was the green-keeper on Machrihanish golf course for many years. When he retired, the captain of the club organised a dinner and provided champagne.
The local minister, who was sitting beside Duncan, noticed that he was not drinking his champagne.
"Don't you like champagne, Duncan?"
"Not verra weel — it's a kind of sour beer," said Duncan.

Later, when the whisky appeared, Duncan said to the minister:
"I think I'll just change to whisky — they continental mineral waters are very lowering."

There was a certain Scottish minister who greatly enjoyed a formal dinner. He was frequently invited because of his standing in his local community. It often fell to his lot to say Grace before the meal started.

When asked to do so he invariably examined the menu with great care and then, according to the detail of the repast provided, started his Grace either:

"Oh Bounteous Lord," or

"Merciful Gawd."

The Duke of Buccleuch and Queensberry, K.T., Formerly, as Earl of Dalkeith, M.P. for Edinburgh North.

The story relates to travel (British Rail), probably the Highland line:
Young lady to guard: "Please, please stop the train!"
Guard: "Why?"
Young lady: "I'm going to have a baby."
Guard: "You had no business to get on the train in that condition."
Young lady: "I wasn't in that condition when I got on the train."

Captain David Buchan of Auchmacoy, J.P., Chief of Buchan Clan.

I was only recently motoring in South Africa when I came to a major road right in the middle of nowhere. Seeing there was nothing coming, I crept round the corner only to be confronted with a vast Boer policeman who stopped me. He soon realised I couldn't understand a word of Afrikaans, so he pulled himself up to his full height, drew out his notebook and rattled off in his best English:

"What is your name in capital letters?"

Later, when I explained why I hadn't stopped at the intersection but only paused, he said, pointing to the road sign:

"That sign says stop, 'S-T-O-P'; had the authorities wanted you to pause they would have put up a different sign saying pause, 'P-A-W-S'."

Lord Campbell of Eskan,
Chairman, Milton Keynes Development Corporation.

A shy curate with a slight stammer — a beginner at golf — asked the secretary of his club whether he could arrange a game for him. The secretary suggested an attractive girl on the practice ground, saying:

"Why don't you go and see if she would give you a game? But, like yourself, she has a slight impediment in her speech."

The curate duly went and made himself known to the girl and they set off in comparative silence. After a couple of holes, he said:

"M-m-my n-n-name's P-P-Peter. B-b-but I'm afraid I'm n-n-not a s-s-saint."

To which the girl replied:

"M-m-my n-n-name's M-M-Mary. And I'm afraid I'm n-n-not a v-v-v-v-v-v-v-v...ery good golfer."

The Archbishop of Canterbury,
(The Most Rev. and Rt. Hon. Robert A.K. Runcie, M.C., D.D.).

Scene: A cocktail party.

Lady to doctor specialist: "You remember me, don't you?"

Specialist (thinking he recognised a one-time patient): "I remember your face, but what else was wrong with you?"

Lord Caradon, P.C., G.C.M.G., K.C.V.O., O.B.E.,
Formerly British Representative at the U.N.

After the vote in the U.N. Security Council, when Deputy Foreign Minister of the Soviet Union, Kuznetsov, voted for the Non-Proliferation Resolution:

When prospects are dark and hopes are dim,
We know that we must turn to him.
When storms and tempests fill the sky,
Bring on Kuznetsov, is the cry.

He comes like a dove from the Soviet Ark,
And light appears where all was dark.

His coming quickly turns the tide;
The propaganda floods subside.
And now that he has changed the weather
Lion and lamb can vote together.

God bless the Russian delegation,
I waive consecutive translation.

Sir Olaf Caroe, K.C.S.I., K.C.I.E., Governor, N.W. Frontier Province, India, 1946–47.

David Somervell, scion of the famous Quaker family that founded 'K' shoes at Kendall, Cumbria, was the eldest son of a Harrow schoolmaster and did the well-known abridgement of the *Great History* by Arnold Toynbee. David was also a notable wit, in a solemn way.

He had been a master at Tonbridge School. On retirement he went to close-by Benenden, a well-known girls' school. On being asked what it was like at Benenden, he replied:

"Like a calm in a teacup."

Sir Hugh Casson, K.C.V.O., P.R.A., Architect.

Doctor: "I fear you have a weakness in the brain..."
Patient: "I'd like a second opinion..."
Doctor: "All right...you're bloody ugly too."

Lord Champion, P.C., J.P.,
Deputy Speaker, Deputy Chairman of Committees, House of Lords.

Lord Haldane had developed something of a pot, which Churchill, then a rather brash young Cabinet colleague, poked with his finger and asked Haldane what he was going to call it. Haldane replied:

"If it's a boy I shall call him George, after His Majesty the King. If it's a girl, Mary, after Her Gracious Majesty the Queen, but if it's only wind, I shall call it Winston."

Sir Joseph Cleary, J.P.,
Hon. Freeman, City of Liverpool.

Chairman (eulogising guest speaker): "His integrity has never been questioned."

Muttered interjection: "It's never even been mentioned."

At a dinner the speaker referred to the three Armed Services and described the Air Force as the Cinderella. The R.A.F. speaker, replying, mentioned that Cinderella had two very ugly sisters.

Lord Cledwyn of Penrhos, P.C., C.H.,
Former Minister of Agriculture; Welsh Secretary.

A visitor to Washington rang President Roosevelt's minister and asked if the President was expected to attend church the following Sunday.

"I cannot promise that," said the minister. "However, I have every expectation that God will be there, and that should be sufficient incentive for a reasonably good attendance."

Tom Sheridan, son of the famous playwright, and a politician, was selected as Parliamentary candidate for a Cornish borough and told his father that, if he won the election, he would stick a label on his forehead with the words 'TO LET', and side with the party that made the best offer.

"You do that, Tom," said Sheridan, "but don't forget to add the word 'UNFURNISHED'."

Sir Alec Clegg,
Formerly Chief Education Officer, West Riding County Council.

Certain areas of local government are known to permit canvassing. In one such area, one candidate wrote personally to every member of the appointing committee. When the chairman of the committee sought to rebuke him, the candidate pointed to the fact that canvassing in the area concerned was known to be commonplace.

This was too much for the chairman who said:

"It is one thing to knock at the door of opportunity; it is quite another to kick in the panel."

By a gravestone in a South Yorkshire village churchyard, a widow was mourning the loss of her second husband.

A former admirer of hers, seeing her distress, sought to comfort her by putting his arm around her, at which she said:

"Take thee 'and off my shoulder; if thee 'ad 'ad any guts, thee'd a' been number one on yon stone."

George Clouston,
Director, London Broadcasting Ltd.; Formerly Musical Director, BBC.

All of his life, a dignified English barrister-widower, with considerable income, had dreamed of playing Sandringham, and one day made up his mind to chance it, although he was well aware that it was very exclusive. When he asked the secretary at the desk if he might play the course, the secretary enquired:

"Member?"

"No, sir."

"Guest of a member?"

"No, sir."

"Sorry," the secretary said.

As he turned to leave, the lawyer spotted a slightly familiar figure seated in the lounge reading *The Times*. It was Lord Wellesby Partham. He approached and, bowing low, said:

"I beg your pardon, your Lordship, my name is Higginbottom of the London firm of Higginbottom, Willoughby and Barclay. I should like to ask you a great favour, sir, whether I might play this delightful course of yours as your guest?"

His Lordship gave Higginbottom a long look, put down his paper and asked:

"Church?"

"Episcopalian, sir, and my wife Church of England."

"Education?"

"Eton, sir, and Oxford. Magna Cum Laude."

"Athletics?"

"Rugby, sir, spot of tennis, and rowed No. 4 on the crew that beat Cambridge."

"Military?"

"D.C.C.E., sir, Coldstream Guards, Victoria Cross, Knight of the Garter."

"Campaigns?"

"Dunkirk, El Alamein, Normandy, sir."

"Languages?"

"Private tutor in French, fluent German, and a bit of Greek, sir."

His Lordship considered briefly, nodded to the secretary and said: "NINE HOLES."

**Air Vice-Marshal Cresswell M. Clementi, C.B., C.B.E.,
Administrator of Sion College, London.**

For those who rather fancy their ability as after-dinner speakers, there is the cautionary tale of the prima donna who was banging on a bit about the fact that her voice was insured for a quarter of a million pounds.

"Oh really," said a bored member of her unimpressed audience, "and what did you do with the money?"

**Sir Robert Cockburn, K.B.E., C.B.,
Civil Servant.**

The teacher was telling her class about the Apollo moon landings. The little boy in the front row was very knowledgeable and kept interrupting.

"The astronauts took off from Cape Canaveral..."

"Miss, they don't take off, they blast off."

"Then they flew off to the moon..."

"Miss, they don't fly, they go into orbit."

"When they landed..."

"Miss, it's only the lunar module that lets down."

The teacher finished the lesson with relief, only to find that the little boy had stayed behind. She waited with apprehension. He slid his hand into hers.

"Miss, Father Christmas does live on the moon, doesn't he?"

Serendipity is going down to the library to take out a book and taking out the librarian instead.

At a critical stage of the war, the Chief of the Air Staff and his two colleagues had spent half an hour with Churchill pleading the cause of Bomber Command. As they left, Lord Hankey said:

"There go three men with but a single thought."

"If that," growled Churchill.

At an R.A.F. conference on the future, the scientists tried to convince the top brass of the value of the vertical take-off aircraft, but without much success. So one of them told the story of the two caterpillars. They were quietly crawling along through the grass, when over them flew a butterfly. One caterpillar turned to the other and said:

"You know, old boy, they'll never get me up in one of those damn things."

The concept of a nuclear deterrent, credible only if never used, is difficult to appreciate. It can be of some help to remember the story of the American who went into Coke's in St. James's for an umbrella. He selected a superb example of the umbrella maker's art.

"Now you must show me how to roll it up."

"Oh, sir! You must never unroll it."

"But what do I do if it rains?"

"Then, sir, you stand on the kerb, raise it in your hand, and shout 'Keb!'."

Sir Barnett Cocks, K.C.B., O.B.E., Clerk of the House of Commons, 1962–73.

In the House of Commons there is a green baize bag which hangs behind the Speaker's Chair. It is intended for public petitions, which are usually great scrolls of parchment, signed by a Member of Parliament and by thousands of his constituents.

One night, after a party of schoolchildren had been escorted through the lobbies, a messenger brought me an anonymous scrap of paper which he had found in the bottom of the Petitions Bag. It read:

'Wot about school dinners?'

Professor Paul M. Cohn, F.R.S., Professor of Mathematics, University of London (Bedford College).

At the time of the political upheavals in Mozambique a few years ago, a social survey organisation in this country put some questions to the man in the street, to see how well informed he was about the situation.

The results revealed an appalling state of ignorance; at least one person questioned thought that 'Lourenço Marques' was one of the Marx Brothers.

This news item from *The Times* was reprinted in the Russian magazine *Za Rubezhom*, with the helpful footnote: "Marx Brothers: a well known London department store."

Professor John P. Corbett,
Professor of Philosophy, University of Bradford, 1972–76.

A distinguished Scottish professor was as absent-minded as professors are supposed to be. He was also a very untidy dresser, and besides the suit that he wore on special occasions possessed, so far as his wife knew, only one pair of trousers.

One morning, soon after he had left to give his lecture, she found to her horror that the suit was in the cupboard and that horrid pair of trousers hanging over the back of his chair. She rushed to the telephone and told the police that Professor X must be walking to the university in his underpants. The patrol car caught him at the entrance to the university arrayed in a splendid new pair of trousers. The constable explained his errand with embarrassment.

"Ah!" said the professor, with a wink, "I am about to lecture on God, and He must have provided."

John Howard Cordle,
Formerly Conservative Member of Parliament for 18 years.

A useful 'Grace' for formal and informal occasions:
"Prevent us, O Lord, from being stodgy and hard to stir like porridge. Please make us more like cornflakes, 'ready to serve'."

The politician has a great regard for himself, little regard for others and no regard for the truth!

Mae West once said: "To err is human and feels divine."

The modest bordering on the lie!
The undertaker, when asked his profession, said:
"I follow the *medical* profession."

38

Raymond Cory,
Chairman, Family Company

Shortly after I joined H.M.S.
King George V in 1942, as a
seaman, I was detailed to a storing
party on the forward gangway. We
were taking supplies from the store
ship, the *Dunluce Castle* across Scapa
Flow. Handling the frozen carcases of
meat from the bottom of the gangway,
I dropped a pig which bobbed off down the side of the ship. I ran up the
gangway, past my colleagues, raced aft to the quarterdeck, saluting,
grabbed a boathook and went down the after gangway waiting for the pig.

Presently a voice from above said:

"Below there! What are you doing?"

I looked up. The Marine Officer-of-the-Day was leaning over the
gangway with his telescope tucked under his arm.

"I'm fishing for a pig, sir."

"Don't skylark. By God, you have caught one! What are you going to do
with it?"

"Well, sir, if you would help..."

"What! Over the Admiral's gangway? Never! Let it go."

Crestfallen, I climbed the gangway and Admiral Sir John Tovey, C.-in-C.
the Home Fleet, was standing watching the proceedings. I think, I hope, I
detected a smile on his face, for it cost me thirty shillings at defaulters the
next day.

Lieut.-General Sir John Cowley, G.C., K.B.E., C.B.,
Formerly Chairman of Various Companies and Schools.

I play a weekly game of golf with an old Irish doctor. Recently he was
taken off to hospital with a serious illness. He recovered and returned home
and I rang him up to welcome him back. I said:

"If life were a game of golf we would both be putting on the eighteenth
green."

He replied:

"The trouble is that, as usual, I've missed my bloody putt — that's why I'm still alive."

Major-General Frank W.J. Cowtan, C.B.E., M.C., Recently Commandant, the Royal Military College of Science.

A very young but somewhat arrogant subaltern arrived in the desert to join the Yorkshire battalion with which I was serving in 1942. He was allotted an orderly who didn't much like his attitude. We 'stood to' in our defensive positions 30 minutes before first light every morning. The next morning the orderly shook the new officer awake in the bottom of his slit trench and said:

"Did you want waking at 0500?"

The officer pulled himself out of his blankets, put on his boots, stuffed on his revolver and got ready for 'stand to'. The orderly quietly watched him doing this and then went on to say:

"Well, it's just gone half past one, sir."

Air Vice-Marshal Joseph Cox, C.B., O.B.E., D.F.C., (Retired), Air Officer Commanding, R.A.F., Ceylon, 1952–55.

A bishop decided to see how a certain lay reader at a church in his diocese was getting on. So, by prior arrangement with the vicar, he attended the church for a Sunday service.

The service went well and towards the end of his address, the lay reader leant forward in the pulpit and said:

"My brethren, I want you to know that some of the happiest moments of my life have been spent in the arms of another man's wife." He quickly spotted that the congregation was shocked, so he added:

"I am, of course, referring to my mother." Sighs of relief from the congregation.

The bishop thought this was wonderful and told the vicar that it was just what he wanted for his address to the Women's Guild in his cathedral in two weeks' time.

A fortnight later his cathedral was packed with these women. The service went well and, when he was about halfway through his address, the bishop said to himself, "Now is the time to throw that in." So he leant forward in the pulpit and said:

"My sisters! I want you to know that some of the happiest moments of my life have been spent in the arms of another man's wife."

All the women were taken aback — shocked! The atmosphere was icy cold. The bishop stood there with a glassy stare in his eyes. After a few moments he leant further forward and said:

"For the life of me I can't remember who she was!"

**Lord Crathorne,
Fine Art Consultant and Lecturer.**

A fisherman's prayer which is engraved on a village church gravestone in Devon:

> God grant that I may fish
> Until my dying day
> And when it comes to my last cast
> I humbly pray,
> When in the Lord's safe landing net
> I'm peacefully asleep
> That in His mercy
> I be judged as good enough to keep.

**Brigadier Sir Douglas Crawford, C.B., D.S.O., T.D., D.L.,
First Lord Lieutenant, Merseyside (Retired).**

A diner at a dinner, at the end of the room, after rather a number of boring speeches and toasts got up and said:

"Mr. Chairman, we have had a number of speeches tonight and a number of toasts, may I have your permission to propose another? I should like to propose 'ABSENT FRIENDS', coupled with the name of the wine waiter who has not been round this end of the table for two hours."

Sir Robert Crichton,
Retired Judge.

The scene is set in the doorway of a manse in Scotland. The time is near
midnight. The snow is falling. The minister, in his nightshirt — wheeshling
around his ankles in the shrill wind — opens the door. He sees a parish-
ioner, Donald Heggie. The following dialogue ensues:

Donald: "Minister, I canna sleep."

Minister: "Well awa' ye to the doctor. It's no business of mine that ye
canna sleep."

, Donald: "Aye, it is your business, minister, for I canna sleep for thinking
of the awful schisms in the Kirk of God."

Minister: "Aye, Donald, 'tis an awful thing to think of the schisms in the
Kirk of God. But this is no time to discuss them. Awa' ye to yer bed and
come here to the manse at four o'clock tomorrow afternoon and we'll have
a good crack about the schisms in the Kirk of God — but mind ye come
sober!"

Donald: "Minister, it'll be no good. For when I'm sober I dinna give a
damn about the schisms in the Kirk of God."

Brigadier Allen Lepard Crockford, C.B.E., D.S.O., M.C., T.D.,
Secretary, St. Thomas's Hospital Medical School, 1946–64.

A party of American tourists were being shown around the Houses of
Parliament. Suddenly, down one of the long corridors, they saw
approaching the Lord Chancellor's procession. As it got close to them
Lord Hailsham caught sight of a friend behind them. Raising his arm he
called out "Neil!", and they all knelt.

Air Commodore Roy Crompton, O.B.E., (Retired),
Commandant, R.A.F. Central Flying School, 1972–74; Currently a Director
at the Home Defence College.

Between the wars in a remote village a coroner was summing up the case
for the benefit of the jury.

"And, if you are satisfied beyond reasonable doubt," he concluded,
"that the victim did, in fact, shoot himself with the gun, it is your duty in
law to return a verdict of felo de se."

The jury was absent for some hours. On its return, the question on reaching a verdict having been put, the foreman replied:

"Yes, sir, we have. We agree with you that the victim did, in fact, shoot himself with the gun — but as you said, he fell in the sea, and we return a verdict of 'Found drowned'."

Rear-Admiral George Clement Crowley, C.B., D.S.C. and Bar, Director-General, Naval Personal Services, 1966–68.

After the war, when at Durban, I was told to take back one million pounds of gold. In due course a funny little man called and explained the situation to me. The number of boxes of gold was considerable.

I decided that I should place them in one of the magazines and I had a special awning arrangement placed under the gangway or brow. Each box was heavy. After some time all the boxes were embarked, the magazine locked and the key given to me. The little man then came into my cabin and asked for a signature for receiving one million pounds of gold for passage to the United Kingdom. I explained to him that I could not very well sign as all I knew was that we had embarked a large quantity of heavy boxes — clearly I did not know positively whether the boxes were really full of gold or not. We had evidently reached an impasse. Finally he said to me:

"If you lose only one of these boxes you won't be able to pay for it." Eventually, after a drink or two, I decided to sign. I then had the best part of six weeks to decide how to handle the affair when I got back to Devonport, which of course we did.

A smallish van, escorted by two policemen, then arrived at the ship and a gentleman from, he said, the Bank of England, came to my cabin. I said that before we started to disembark he must, of course, be prepared to sign that he had received so many boxes of gold. He then said that this was quite impossible. Whereupon I said that unless he signed, or I was ordered by the C.-in-C., I could not possibly start unloading.

Drink, you know, is a wonderful morale raiser, because after two — or was it three? — he signed and all the gold was eventually disembarked.

That is the closest I have ever been to being, at least temporarily, a millionaire.

Professor Alexander Cullen, O.B.E., F.R.S.,
Senior Research Fellow, Electronics, University College, London.

The late Lord Jackson, a former President of the Institution of Electrical Engineers, told a delightful story of a brief encounter with a forthright Manchester tram conductress in his early days as an apprentice at Metropolitan Vickers.

One day, soon after he had joined the company, he overslept. He dressed hastily, rushed out and jumped on a tram just as it was gathering speed. He collapsed breathless onto a seat, and when the conductress came round the following conversation took place:

"Trafford Park."

"We're not going to Trafford Park."

"But it says Trafford Park on the side."

"Yes, luv, but we're not going sideways."

Roland Culver,
Actor.

In my youth the nefarious machinations of milkmen were well worn music-hall jokes, but this story never reached the boards.

In those days the milkman would carry a two-gallon can of milk to the tradesman's entrance and with a half-pint ladle pour the amount ordered into china jugs supplied by the cook. One of the tricks these cunning fellows had was to add water to the milk, thus diddling the dairy and the customer, both.

My mother considered that the milk was becoming very diluted and complained to cook. Cook said:

"Yes, madam, Mr. Evans (the milkman) is certainly watering it. What's more, he's giving us short measure."

"Very well," said my mama, "call me to the door tomorrow and I will tackle Mr. Evans."

On the morrow mother confronted Mr. Evans and said:

"Mr. Evans, not only have you been diluting our milk but you have been giving short measure."

Mr. Evans replied indignantly:

"Oh no, ma'am, I wouldn't do you *both* ways."

Sir James Currie, K.B.E., C.M.G., Formerly of H.M. Diplomatic Service.

A young official from one of the emerging states in Africa was sent to me to get some experience. That was easy, for I was then posted to a country where colour was no barrier. My only doubt was his reception by a small local white community. I need not have worried. They took to him and he to them. When he was leaving some of them gave him a farewell dinner.

Next morning I asked him how it went.

"Marvellous," he replied, "if I could, I would have blushed."

Vice-Admiral Sir John Cuthbert, K.B.E., C.B., D.L., Flag Officer Scotland, 1956–58.

Between the wars an admiral wrote the following report on his flag captain.

"This officer has that quality which, in myself, I consider firmness of purpose, but in him bloody obstinacy."

Footnote: They both became Admirals of the Fleet.

Many years ago, in London, I used to exercise my black labrador and my black dachshund before breakfast. One morning a night watchman's hut had appeared and as I passed, outward bound, there was an audible sucking of teeth from the occupant. Twenty minutes later, on my return journey, there was a further tooth suck and the comment:

"Worn that one's legs down a bit, haven't you."

Dr. Lionel Dakers, F.R.C.O., Director of the Royal School of Church Music.

During the time I was organist of Exeter Cathedral, a couple of Americans arrived to visit the cathedral late on a Saturday evening. Told by the verger that the cathedral was about to close but would be open again at seven o'clock in the morning, the husband turned to his wife and remarked:

"Say, what d'yer know; this place even opens on a Sunday."

In the Church of England, 'A Table of Kindred and Affinity' tells you exactly whom you may, or may not, marry. It is frequently to be seen displayed in the porchyard of a church. In a certain Sussex village church, underneath the statement which says: "A man may not marry his mother-in-law", someone had written:

"Lord have mercy upon us and incline our hearts to keep this law."

**Sir Alan Dalton, C.B.E.,
Deputy Chairman, English China Clays Ltd.**

I heard recently of a young man who had been trying for hours unsuccessfully to extract an overdraft from his bank manager. Almost at the end of his patience, the bank manager finally said to the applicant:

"I am a sporting man — you have tried hard; I am still not impressed. I have a glass eye. If you can guess which one it is, you can have your loan!"

Without any hesitation whatsoever the young man said:

"It is your left eye!"

The bank manager was astonished, and said:

"I have asked that question hundreds of times and no one has ever got it right before. How did you guess?"

"It's a damn sight more sympathetic than your right," said the young man!

A young businessman was looking for a bright, buttoned-up and bushy-tailed Girl Friday-type, but was concerned how he was going to sift through the long list of applicants that had replied to his advertisement. He consulted a friend, who was in the personnel selection field, who offered to help. With his vast experience he was able to whittle down the list to three, whom he proposed to the young businessman that he should call for interviews.

"That's all very well, but how shall I discover if they are made of the right material?" asked the businessman.

"That's easy," replied his friend. "Ask each one of them what she would do if she was shipwrecked, and after swimming around for several hours, she came across an island which was inhabited only by men — 40 of them!"

When the interviews commenced, the question was duly asked of the first young lady. She replied that she thought she would swim away and try to find another island. The second one answered that she would climb ashore and find the largest and strongest man and seek him out as her protector. The third one said:

"I've heard the question — where's the problem?"

Professor Peter Victor Danckwerts, G.C., M.B.E., F.R.S.,
Emeritus Professor of Chemical Engineering, Cambridge University.

The scene is the Portsmouth Hippodrome on a Saturday night.

An ageing beauty in a big hat sings sentimental ballads. Uproar, jeers and shouts of "Get off!". A burly stoker rises in the gallery and yells out:

"Shut up! Give the poor old cow a chance!"

She looks up with melting eyes.

"Thank you, sir. At least there's one gentleman in the house."

Major-General Brian Daunt, C.B., C.B.E., D.S.O.,
Formerly Controller, Home Department, British Red Cross Society, 1957-66.

The Law Society in Plymouth had kindly invited me to a dinner in honour of the Lord Chief Justice, Lord Goddard.

They had previously dined him in the same hotel when he was the circuit judge; the memory was bitter in their minds, for there had been an unfortunate incident with the wine — on putting the claret to his lips their guest had said: "Filth" and turned to the wine waiter demanding whisky instead.

There must be no mistake this time: their most knowledgeable wine bibber, a Mr. X, was detailed to select claret and port of the finest vintage. I happened to be sitting next to him; he was trembling with apprehension; the moment my glass was filled, he said:

"Quick, tell me if it's all right." I lifted the glass, it was a very deep colour. I took one sip, put the glass down and said:

"It's the port."

Mr. X rushed up the table hoping to get to Lord Goddard before he touched it: alas, he was too late. He stood horrified waiting for the explosion — but the Lord Chief Justice knew his wine. He wasn't going to throw away a whole claret glass of vintage port. He pushed it forward saying:

"Very good, I'll keep that for later."

Aubrey C. Davidson-Houston,
Portrait Painter.

A secretary of a golf club, noticing an argument going on between three players on the eighteenth green, with a fourth player lying on the ground, went out to see what was happening. He said:

"Gentlemen, gentlemen, what is all this fuss? Will somebody tell me what the argument is about?"

A little man said:

"Yes, I'll tell you. My partner and I — that's him on the ground — were all square with our opponents when we reached this green, and then I'm afraid my partner had a stroke, and now the other two want to count it."

Sir David Davenport-Handley, O.B.E., J.P., D.L.,
Former Chairman, National Union of Conservative & Unionist Associations.

Definition of a Conference:
A gathering whose members singly can do nothing, but who together decide that nothing can be done.

Definition of a Committee:
The appointment of the unfit and the unwilling to do the unnecessary.

Sir Alun Davies, Q.C.,
Recorder and Honorary Recorder of the City of Cardiff.

Clerk of the court: "And how do you plead, guilty or not guilty?"
Defendant in the dock: "Not *very* guilty."

Major-General Sir James d'Avigdor-Goldsmid, Bt., C.B., O.B.E., M.C.,
Army 1932–68; M.P. 1970–74.

What do you get if you pour boiling water down a rabbit hole?
A hot cross bun.

Sir Charles Davis, C.B.,
Second Counsel to the Speaker, House of Commons.

There once was a famous High Court judge of whom it was said, on his death, that he ought to have left his liver to the nation.

Air Chief Marshal Sir John Davis, G.C.B., O.B.E., Lieutenant-Governor of Jersey, 1969–74.

The Pope died and went to heaven. He was very graciously received by St. Peter and conducted to dignified lodgings where he was suitably received and entertained; nothing ostentatious, but all very pleasant. He went to bed early but was awakened next morning by a tremendous noise. He went to the window and looked out. The streets were thronged with cheering people, the ticker-tape was coming down thickly, and there was a scene of the greatest enthusiasm. Down the main street was coming an open car and standing in the back was an Air Chief Marshal in full uniform raising his arms above his head in acknowledgement of all the cheering. The excitement was terrific.

St. Peter happened to come in at this moment and the Pope, who was a very holy man — not at all given to pride and jealousy — said to him:

"St. Peter, don't think I am complaining in any way about my treatment here — you have been most kind — but after all, I was the Pope, and what has that fellow done to deserve the reception he is getting?"

St. Peter laughed and said:

"Well, it's like this, Your Holiness. According to my calculations you are the 149th Pope we've had here, but that is the first Air Chief Marshal!"

Jersey is a great place for cattle and there are frequent agricultural shows where all the prize cattle compete against each other. As Lieutenant-Governor I used to go very often to these shows and the form was that I would drive up and be welcomed by the committee and conducted into the prize ring to meet the judges and view the scene.

On one occasion I did this and as I entered the ring the loud-speaker was just announcing the next class to be judged. It went like this:

"And the next class to be judged, ladies and gentlemen, is Aged Bulls," — very slight pause — "and we are very glad to welcome His Excellency the Lieutenant-Governor!"

50

Sir Alan Dawtry, C.B.E., T.D.,
Formerly Chief Executive, Westminster City Council.

An uncle of mine, now dead from cirrhosis of the liver, emigrated to Canada. The first thing he saw there on landing was a sign which said 'Drink Canada Dry'. This, during the ensuing years, is what he tried to do.

A schoolboy wrote to his parents about the school play, which unfortunately they had missed.

"The play," he wrote, "was 'Hamlet'. Most of the parents had seen it before but they laughed just the same."

At the funeral of a woman just outside Paris, her young lover was seen sobbing inconsolably by the graveside. When the ceremony was over the dead woman's husband walked over to the young man, patted him on the back and said:

"Please don't take it so hard. Perhaps I'll marry again."

Colonel Donald Dean, V.C., O.B.E., T.D., D.L., J.P.,
Deputy Lieutenant for Kent, 1957.

A lady cathedral guide spotted a woman entering the sacred building wearing a bikini; uncertain what to do about it she hurried to consult an elderly canon who said: "Tell her to take it off."

**Viscount De L'Isle, V.C., K.G., P.C., G.C.M.G., G.C.V.O.,
Chairman, Freedom Association.**

One fine spring day I was speaking to a group of school children in a small town in Western Australia. I told them:

"You are lucky to live in such a beautiful countryside, truly 'a land flowing with milk and honey'." (Exodus Ch. 3 v. 8.)

"Where does that come from?" I asked a small girl.

"Cows and bees," came the unhesitating reply.

**Professor Donald Robert Denman,
Professor Emeritus of Land Economy, Cambridge University.**

It was the run up to Christmas; even the dons of Cambridge were having parties and in the village of Coton, some twelve miles out of the city, the party was in full swing. Not until the guests were on the point of departure did the hosts realise that the heavens had opened; visibility was down to ten yards, diminished by the sheer intensity of what the Germans would call 'string rain'.

The Professor of Moral Theology, slightly bowed, white haired and happy, was still supping his port. The hostess whispered to her husband:

"We can't let him go home in this." The husband agreed and, pointing to the rain, invited the professor to stay the night. Soon the other guests claimed his attention and an hour passed before the last bade farewell. At that point the hostess realised that she had lost the professor. They couldn't find him anywhere.

Later on, well into the small hours, there was a knock at the front door. There stood the professor drenched in rain, clutching a parcel.

"May I come in?" he said. "I went back to Cambridge to fetch my pyjamas."

**Sir Robert Dent, C.B.,
Formerly Clerk of Public Bills, House of Commons.**

Mother (at the end of an attempt to persuade her daughter to walk to the local town to save fuel):

"After all, what were you given two legs for?"

"Oh," cried the daughter, "one for the accelerator and one for the brake."

R. Beresford Dew,
Professor of Management, Sciences, Manchester University.

A young naval officer went down the breakwater for a swim, but just as he was about to dive in he noticed a large jellyfish. The jellyfish spoke to him and said:

"I shouldn't dive in here, sir, it's very rocky, there is a much better place lower down."

He thanked the jellyfish, went for a delightful swim and, as he was returning, thought; "that's a very strange thing about that jellyfish," so he went back and engaged the jellyfish in conversation.

The jellyfish explained that it was rather a long story, but in short, it wasn't really a jellyfish but a beautiful WRN, only she was under a magic spell. The only way the spell could be broken would be to put the jellyfish, at the witching hour, on somebody's pillow and it would immediately turn back into a beautiful WRN. He said he would be delighted to help and put the jellyfish, which was very wet and slippery of course, into his mackintosh pocket, returned to his ship and, at the witching hour, put the jellyfish carefully onto his pillow.

Unfortunately, at the court martial they didn't believe this story about the jellyfish.

Peter Dickinson,
Composer and Pianist; Professor of Music at Keele University.

My father, the late Frank Dickinson, who pioneered the development of contact lenses, was walking along the beach at Lytham St. Anne's. The town is on the estuary of the river Ribble, in Lancashire, and at the Lytham end of it there are usually several small boats moored on the shore.

It was early one Sunday morning and my father was looking to see what the tide had brought in. As it happened, the previous night had been memorable for a particularly intense storm. Ahead of him he saw a man with some rope and what appeared to be some planks of good quality wood. Since my father liked picking up things on the beach himself he congratulated the apparently successful beachcomber.

"You've got some fine timber there, haven't you?"

"Timber? That's my bloody boat!"

Major-General Roy L.C. Dixon, C.B., M.C.,
Formerly Chief of Staff, Allied Forces, Northern Europe.

A Japanese delegation visiting Israel announced their wish to lay a wreath on the tomb of the Unknown Soldier. Since such a thing does not exist in Israel and not wishing to disappoint the delegation, Golda Meir directed that the wreath should be laid on the most impressive tomb available, which happened to be that of Mendelssohn. All went well until one of the Japanese Embassy staff, who could read the inscription in Hebrew, pointed out that this was not the Unknown Soldier's tomb but indeed Mendelssohn's. Golda Meir was unruffled.

"That is perfectly true," she quickly replied. "Mendelssohn was a very great composer, but as a soldier he was absolutely unknown."

Sir Douglas Dodds-Parker,
Formerly Sudan Political Service.

At a diplomatic party there were two couples each with the name of Williams. It happened that Mr. Williams 'A' was talking to Mrs. Williams 'B' when a nervous secretary introduced them to the Foreign Minister thus:

"This is Mr. and Mrs. Williams — who are not married."

Perplexed doctor to patient: "Have you ever had this before?"
Patient: "Yes."
Doctor: "Well, you've got it again."

Professor Gordon Donaldson, F.R.S.E., F.B.A.,
H.M. Historiographer in Scotland.

There was once a professor who scored a double triumph on the same day and who might have been, as the Melrose Chronicler said of Alexander II, *duplici gaudio exhillaratus*. His wife gave birth to twins and his long-awaited *magnum opus* at last saw the light of day.

When he went into the lecture theatre next morning to meet his large class, his students, who had heard about the twins, greeted him with loud applause. (It was in the days when students were much more demonstrative than they are now.)

The professor, whose mind was running entirely on the achievement of his publication, protested:

"Thank you, gentlemen, thank you. I appreciate your congratulations. But I assure you I could never have achieved this without the active co-operation of my colleagues in the department."

A country minister, on a very small stipend, was unexpectedly offered the chance to move to a wealthy city parish. One of his congregation, who had heard of this, called at the manse, where he was met by the minister's daughter. He asked her if her father had come to a decision.

"Well, daddy's in the study praying for guidance, and mummy's upstairs packing."

Robert Dougall, M.B.E., Author and Broadcaster; Formerly Senior BBC TV Newsreader.

The Soviet Head of State, Leonid Brezhnev, was showing his aged mother the delights of Moscow.

First, he showed her his splendid apartments in the Kremlin, then his dozen super motor cars, and finally took her to the Bolshoi Theatre where they sat in the former Czar's box. Being up from the country, the old lady seemed dazed by the magnificence.

"It's all very wonderful Leonid, but there's one thing worrying me — what will you do when the revolution comes?"

Major-General Arthur J.H. Dove, C.B., C.B.E.,
War Office Representative with the Council of Foreign Ministers.

Ernest Bevin was chatting about different trades after dinner one evening and asked me whether I had studied their psychology. He illustrated his point in the following way.

"Take bus drivers and tram drivers. They are quite different. The bus driver has to cope with traffic all day. He gets irritated by having to weave in and out of other drivers and getting held up in traffic jams. He finishes up thoroughly irritable. Now I'd never see a deputation of bus drivers in the evening. I'd send them home to work it off on the old woman and I'd see them in the morning, and they'd talk sense.

"Now the tram driver is quite different. He goes along placidly on his two rails, tinkles his little bell, and everything has to get out of his way. I'd see a deputation of tram drivers at any time, and they'd talk sense!"

Lieut.-Colonel Sir John Dring, K.B.E., C.I.E., J.P., D.L.,
Indian Political Service (Retired).

In the depths of winter, years ago, the newly appointed Governor-General of Canada was due to be welcomed on his arrival in Ottawa. The train drew to a halt opposite the red carpet, some A.D.C.s jumped out, the local dignitaries stood to attention, the guard of honour presented arms and the band prepared to play the National Anthem, but, alas, there was no Governor-General.

He had not been warned of the weather extremes and at the last moment had found his teeth frozen solid in their bathroom glass!

Sir Herbert du Heaume, C.I.F., O.B.E., K.P.M.,
Retired Deputy Inspector-General, Indian Police.

A small niece once asked me why all colonels were left-handed. I asked why she thought they were and she replied:

"Well, they call them left-handed colonels."

Lord Duncan-Sandys, C.H.,
Former Cabinet Minister.

There are three ages of man:
Youth, middle-age, and "How well you look!".

Captain James L. Dunkley, C.B.E., R.D.,
Formerly Commodore, P&O Passenger Services.

As captain of P&O liners one often meets people of interest 'At the Captain's Table'. The most outstanding of these in my career was Sir Eric Harrison, Australian High Commissioner in London. He had a fund of stories and could also quote poetry from the English classics to Australian bush ballads, apparently *ad infinitum*.

What remains in my memory as his best story concerns a Negro on a Southern plantation who announces to his boss one day that his wife has just presented him with their eleventh child. The boss replies:

"Sambo, you should not treat your wife so and you had better see to it that it does not happen again."

"Yes, boss," replies Sambo, "if it happens again I'll hang myself."

But about a year later Sambo has occasion to tell the boss:

"Guess what? My wife has just presented me with number twelve!"

"But I thought you said that if it happened again you would hang yourself."

"Yes, I did, boss, and when it happened I got me a rope and climbed a tall tree. I fastened one end to the tree and the other round my neck and was about to jump when I said to myself: 'Sambo, maybe you's hanging de wrong man'."

Bishop of Durham,
(The Rt. Rev. John Stapylton Habgood, D.D.).

A solitary traveller had fallen over a cliff at night. Luckily he managed to grab hold of a bush near the top, and hung there over the blackness shouting:

"Is anybody down there?"

"Yes," came a voice. "I am down here. Let yourself go. You can trust me. I am God."

There was a long pause.

"Is anybody else down there?"

Sir Alexander Durie, C.B.E.,
Vice-President, The Automobile Association.

Opening remarks by the late Lord Birkett giving an after-dinner speech:

"Gentlemen, the speech you are about to hear I have delivered twice before, once to the Bar Council and once to the inmates of Dartmoor Prison. I would ask any of you who were present on either of those occasions to bear with me."

A salesman tired of his job joined the police force. A friend asked him:

"How do you like being a policeman?"

He replied:

"The pay is good and the hours are O.K. but best of all the customer is always wrong!"

Advertisement by the Prison Department of the Home Office:

"The Modern Prison Service offers free housing..."

Sir Esmond Durlacher,
Member of London Stock Exchange, 1926–77.

Our very Irish cook, who can always
be relied upon to produce a
malapropism, excelled herself at the time
of the last General Election.
Having been asked by my wife to bring
back a pot of honey from the
village, I took it into the kitchen and
asked the cook if what I had got would do.
"Oh, yes, sir," she said, "it must be all right,
it's marked '*pure* honey' so there can't be any conservatives in it."

Sir John Eardley-Wilmot, Bt., M.V.O., D.S.C.,
Staff of Monopolies Commission, since 1967.

A nasty accident happened in a factory in South Wales and one of the
workers was killed. His mates decided that they ought to send somebody
round to tell Mrs. Jones personally and they agreed that the most tactful of
the friends should go. After a great deal of argy-bargy they picked on Dai
the convener.

Dai knocked on the door of the terraced house and said:

"Are you the Widow Jones?"

"I'm not; I sent Jones off this morning with his butties and he was
perfectly all right."

"Want to bet?"

Air Chief Marshal Sir Alfred Earle, G.B.E., C.B.,
Formerly Vice-Chief of Defence Staff.

A bishop was visiting a village in his diocese for a confirmation service.
As the result of unforeseen delays he found it necessary to stay the night at
the village inn. Unfortunately there was no single room available but it was
arranged that he should have a double room to himself.

After a pleasant dinner and a chat in the bar he retired to his room to find the bed neatly turned back with his pyjamas laid out on one side and his surplice on the other!

**Admiral Sir James Eberle, G.C.B.,
Commander-in-Chief, Fleet; Allied Commander-in-Chief, Channel.**

A certain admiral who liked always to have the last word and who was noted for his addiction to work, was walking round his flagship one morning.

In the barber's shop he came upon a sailor in the chair. The use of 'service time' for such an activity was not popular with the admiral.

"Having your hair cut in working hours I see," humphed the admiral.

"Yes, sir, it grew in working hours," replied the sailor.

The admiral was not yet to be outdone.

"It didn't *all* grow in working hours," he said.

"No, sir," responded the sailor, "I'm not having it *all* cut off!"

On 7 December 1941 a British corvette was in the North Atlantic leading the escort of a large U.K.-bound convoy.

The convoy had already been attacked by German submarines and several ships sunk. The ships of the convoy had become somewhat scattered and communications with them in the prevailing gale and heavy seas were very difficult.

The corvette itself had been slightly damaged and was unable to use its weapons. The captain had broken his leg and was turned in down below.

On the bridge the second-in-command faced a bleak prospect. He knew that another submarine pack was between him and the convoy's U.K. destination. The weather was improving but a further severe gale with low visibility was forecast.

In the radio office a secret, Most Immediate, signal was received. It was laboriously decoded and passed urgently to the bridge. The second-in-command read:

"Commence hostilities against Japan."

H.R.H. The Prince Philip, Duke of Edinburgh.

Bishop Launcelot Fleming began his after-dinner speech with the surprising statement that he felt rather like a swan. When the giggles had subsided he went on:

"All calm and serene on the surface, but paddling like anything underneath."

Sir George Edwards, O.M., C.B.E., F.R.S.,
Formerly Chairman of British Aircraft Corporation.

"The British soldier can stand up to anything except the British War Office." — George Bernard Shaw.

John Basil Edwards, C.B.E., J.P.,
Former Chairman, Magistrates' Association.

A farmer's representative was asked on the BBC what he did for recreation. He replied that he went out with his gun, adding:

"I'm very fond of wildlife."

Sir Martin Edwards, D.L.,
A Past President of the Law Society.

The magistrates adjourned the case so that the defendant might be interviewed by the probation officer.

At the adjourned hearing the probation officer reported:

"Your Worships, I found the defendant to be a man of few words, but he gave me the benefit of two of them."

Lord Eliot,
Landowner.

Once upon a time, not so long ago, three tortoises (two big ones and one little one) set out for a picnic. It took a very, very long time indeed for the three of them to reach their intended spot, but happily for them the weather was fine all week. When they arrived the two big ones at once unpacked the eggs, the bread, the biscuits, jams, cakes and a large bottle of fizzy lemonade. Meanwhile, the little one was sent off to forage for suitable green stuff to make a salad.

When he got back the little one was greeted with a gruff voice saying:
"You have forgotten the salt."
"What you mean is, *we* have forgotten the salt, don't you?"
"Well it does not matter one way or the other, you just run along and fetch it and be quick about it."
"Why me?"
"Cos."
"Because why?"
"Because we are bigger than you and we say so, O.K.?"
"O.K.," said the little one resignedly, "I'll go, but only on one condition, that you absolutely promise not to drink the fizzy lemonade."
"Fair enough, now gertcha!"
So off scampered the little one. After a day he was almost completely out of sight and the others sat down to wait. A week went by with no sign of him, as did the rest of the month. By now the big ones were ready for a drink. After a brief discussion they mutually agreed to have just a sip and were about to do so when a little head looked round from a pile of stones and said:
"If you do, I won't go."

George Elrick, F.R.S.A.,
Former President of the Entertainments Agents Association.

Being an Aberdonian, and reputed to be mean, which is a cheap way of advertising ourselves, I tell this story against myself.
A fellow died and went to heaven and Peter said:
"You have been a bad man and can't come in unless you have passed the

test. Take this spoon and go to the desert and turn over every grain of sand."

"That's going to take a long time," said the guy.

"You have plenty of time," said Peter, "you're dead."

So off he went and did it, returning to heaven a hundred years later.

"Now your next test," said Peter. "Are you ready? Take this bucket and turn over every wave in the ocean."

"That's not fair," said the guy, "isn't there an alternative?"

"Well," said Peter, "you could go down to the Savoy Hotel in London. There's a function on tonight and George Elrick is speaking. Stand beside him until he buys you a double scotch."

"Give me the bucket," said the guy.

Mrs. O'Donovan was walking down O'Connell Street, in Dublin, and coming in the opposite direction was Father O'Rafferty.

"Hello," said the Father, "and how's Mrs. O'Donovan, didn't I marry you two years ago?"

"You did that, Father."

"And are there any little ones yet?"

"No, not yet, Father," said she.

"Well now, I'm going to Rome next week, and I'll light a candle for you."

"Thank you, Father," and away she went.

A few years later they met again.

"Well now, Mrs. O'Donovan," said the Father, "how are you?"

"Oh, very well," said she.

"And tell me," he said, "have you any little ones yet?"

"Oh, yes, Father. I've had three sets of twins, and four singles — ten in all."

"Now isn't that wonderful," he said. "And how is your lovely husband?"

"Oh," she said, "he's over in Rome to blow the bloody candle out."

Sir George Erskine, C.B.E.,
Member, Directors' Advisory Committee, Morgan Grenfell & Co. Ltd.

A fishmonger was 'in the red' at his bank. He, being a practical joker, displayed a box labelled 'For the Blind'.

Many months later he put a notice in his window thanking everyone for his 'new blind'.

Major-General Henry Holland Evans, C.B.,
Formerly Director of Army Education.

When I was serving in North Africa I was fascinated by the history and spent a lot of time looking at the Roman remains.

I went to Sabratha and talked to the soldiers there about all the marvellous works, including theatres and markets, which can still be seen.

I was cut down to size by a letter sent by one of the troopers of the 4th/7th Dragoon Guards. It said:

"We had an officer who came to tell us *all* about this place. It is full of camels and wogs. This officer told us that it was built by the Ities before the war."

Some lecturer!

Lord Fairfax of Cameron,
Lawyer.

An Australian lady was driving in England for the first time and had considerable difficulty negotiating her first English roundabout. Unfortunately she got into awful confusion and caused a massive traffic jam. Inevitably the law arrived in the shape of a very fresh-faced and young constable, who explained to the Australian lady that she had committed several traffic offences and that he would have to ask for her name and address.

"Certainly," she replied, "I am Mrs. Farquharson-Colquhoun and I live at Wrai-Wrai, Coppymurambilla, Bogabilla, Gundawindi, New South Wales."

"In that case, madam, drive on."

Sir Roger Falk, O.B.E.,
Deputy Chairman, Gaming Board of Great Britain; Author; Management
Consultant.

Let it never be said that I'm mocking the noble efforts of traditional Indian Babus (clerks) to use the English language to the best of their ability. I shall, however, never forget a letter I got from my chief Babu in Calcutta when I got home to get married in 1938. He was a fine man, now dead, and I loved him. He wrote:

"Dear Sir,

By the time this letter shall have been received by you I, too, hope to be connubially pinned to a paramour of mine. God bless you.

Yours, etc."

'Connubially pinned' seems to me to describe the marriage condition (in certain cases) admirably!

Lieut.-Colonel Sir Peter Farquhar, Bt., D.S.O. and Bar, J.P.,
Past Chairman, Master of Foxhounds Association; Vice-President, National
Association of Boys' Clubs.

During a lull in the fighting in the Middle East in the last war, my regiment was pulled out of the line for a few days' much needed rest. On the Sunday, the normal procedure would have been a regimental church parade, for which the men would have to smarten themselves up and be marched from each squadron area to Regimental H.Q.

I could not see the sense in this and suggested to our padre that he should go round to each squadron in turn, and hold a short service at which anyone who wanted to attend could do so voluntarily, in whatever state of dress, or undress, he happened to be.

The padre readily agreed and orders went out accordingly; however, the next morning my regimental sergeant major, a truly excellent warrant officer of the old order, went to my adjutant and asked:

"Beg pardon, sir, how many men per squadron shall I detail for the colonel's voluntary church parade?"

Incidentally this procedure, both then and later, proved very popular and produced remarkably high attendances.

Professor John Ferguson,
President, Selly Oak Colleges, Birmingham.

A former Bishop of Guildford was holding a 'retreat' for ordinands, and left them to an afternoon of prayer and meditation. He was somewhat surprised to meet one of them an hour or so later in the streets of Guildford and remarked with some asperity:

"I thought I left you to an afternoon of prayer and meditation!"

The young man replied:

"Yes, my lord, but I received strict instructions from the Holy Spirit that I was to do my shopping this afternoon and I couldn't very well go against the Holy Spirit, could I?"

"Well," said the bishop, "one of you must be wrong, because it's early closing day."

A chairman introduced me with the words:

"Some of you have heard John Ferguson before and some haven't. Those of you who haven't will be looking forward eagerly to hearing him."

Once in America there was a very wealthy self-made devoted Roman Catholic. He had no children and it was assumed that the Church would inherit his money. Suddenly he became interested in giving others the education he had missed, and was speaking of endowing the local Liberal Arts College. His priest reported this to the bishop, who said:

"I think I can deal with that."

He went to the millionaire.

"Ah, Mr. so-and-so, I hear you're interested in education. Very commendable. Now this college you're interested in, I suppose you know that the dean's a sexagenarian?"

"He isn't!"

"I can assure you that it is so. And do you realise that the young men and women use the same curriculum?"

"They don't!"

"They do indeed. And the College itself insists that they matriculate together in public."

"Not a cent do they get from me!" said the millionaire.

Professor Henry S. Ferns,
Professor of Political Science, University of Birmingham.

There is an Argentine joke which goes like this. The U.S. Government's Space Agency planned a manned flight to Venus, but could find no American to undertake this assignment. The authorities decided to advertise internationally. Three men applied: an Italian, a Frenchman and an Argentine.

The Italian was examined first and found to be satisfactory: healthy, intelligent, brave and technically proficient. He was asked how much he required by way of pay. He replied:

"A million dollars."

The Frenchman was found to be equally satisfactory, but when asked about pay he replied:

"Two million dollars."

He was then asked to explain why he wanted twice what the Italian had asked. The Frenchman said:

"Like the Italian I want one million as compensation for the ardours of training, my technical expertise and the dangers of the job. I also want a million to enjoy life before I leave, and to provide for my family and friends."

The Argentine was then examined, found in every way to be satisfactory and asked about his pay. He replied that he wanted three million dollars.

"But why?" asked the Americans. "An Italian will do the job for a million. A Frenchman wants two million. Here you are, you want three million. Why?"

"It is simple," replied the Argentine. "There is a million for you, a million for me, and we send the Italian. I'll throw in the launching site free!"

Commander James Buchanan Findlay, C.B.E., R.N. (Retired),
Deputy Governor, Bank of Scotland, until 1971.

A Scots minister called one afternoon on a widow who had a nine-year-old son. After a short conversation the widow said she would put the kettle on.

The minister asked the boy if there was anything he would like explained.
The boy asked:

"What is a miracle?"

The minister did his best in the short time available and then asked the
boy if he now understood what a miracle was.

"Yes," said the boy, "but it's not my mother's idea of a miracle. When she
told me you were calling this afternoon she said it would be a miracle if you
didn't stay for tea."

Seventy years ago a small church in a Highland glen had been
redecorated and improvements made to the organ. Sufficient money had
been raised and the bills paid.

The minister, from the pulpit, thanked the congregation for their interest
and generosity. He then looked at the organ and said that the organist, our
dear Miss Macrae, had told him that due to the fitting of automatic
couplings she could now change her combinations without moving her feet.

An Argyllshire shepherd went all the way to Lanark for a big sheep sale.
That night he tried to book a room. He tried hotel after hotel but they were
all full. Eventually the manager of a small hotel said there was a room with
a double bed with, so far, only a girl in it. So the manager went upstairs and
the girl said she had no objection. The shepherd was taken upstairs, kicked
off his boots and got into bed.

Five minutes later the girl said:

"I'm feeling cold."

"Shut up," said the shepherd. "I am very tired and want to go to sleep."

Five minutes later the girl said:

"Would you shut the window?"

The shepherd — the simple countryman — then had a brilliant idea and
said:

"Shall we pretend to be married?"

The girl said:

"That would be wonderful, just what I was hoping for."

"Well," said the shepherd, "now *you* can get up and shut the ruddy
window."

Professor Antony G.N. Flew,
Professor of Philosophy, University of Reading.

At one time during one of the four presidencies of Franklin Delano Roosevelt, tariffs were the great question of the hour. Two speechwriters came into the Oval Office the day before he was due to address a major rally. One had a text strongly urging across-the-board reductions, the other one arguing with equal strength for correspondingly wholesale increases. They asked him:

"Mr. President, which of these two drafts do you want us to polish up for tomorrow's rally?", to which the old master replied with another question:

"Well, couldn't you just somehow manage to weave the two themes together?"

Professor Gordon Elliott Fogg, F.R.S.,
Professor of Marine Biology, University College of North Wales.

In 1956 I attended an international congress in Helsinki in the company of Professor W.H. Pearsall. On arrival by boat in the morning we were met and taken directly to the university hostel where we were to stay. After dumping our luggage we went straight back into the city to do some sightseeing and it wasn't until late evening that we returned to the hostel. To our consternation it was silent and locked! After we had rung the bell and banged for five minutes or so to no avail, Pearsall produced from his pockets a large bunch of keys, a penknife and a bit of wire, remarking:

"I think I can get us in."

Feeling doubtful about the propriety of this I decided the best thing was to walk round the building and look for a back door. I didn't find one and when I got back there was a small crowd watching Pearsall's attempts to pick the front door lock. None of them spoke English but they were discussing the proceedings in what, for Finns, was a very animated manner. Neither of us knew any Finnish but one word, 'bibliotek', sounded familiar and kept on coming up. Quite suddenly we realised that we were trying to break into the university library and the building next door, with open doors and lights blazing, was our hostel.

I had some difficulty in getting Pearsall away; he was convinced that in another few minutes he would have mastered that lock.

This story was told to me in Madison, Wisconsin. I've never heard anyone else tell it on this side of the Atlantic so I consider that I have the European rights.

A distinguished concert pianist revisited the remote English village where he had spent his boyhood and, of course, was asked to give a recital. Having vivid memories of the village hall and its ancient upright piano he was reluctant, but he eventually allowed himself to be persuaded on the understanding that the instrument would be tuned before he played it. When the time came he was just about to begin playing when his attention was distracted by someone beckoning urgently from the wings. He went over and recognised the mechanic from the local garage, who said:

"I tooned your pianner for you, Guv, but there's one thing you should know — black plays white and white plays black."

The Hon. Sir Peter Foster, M.B.E., T.D., High Court Judge.

Counsel to accused in the dock:
"In what state were you on the night in question?"
Accused: "Drunk as a Judge."
Judge: "Don't you mean 'Drunk as a Lord?'"
Accused: "Yes, my Lord."

Sir Charles Frederick, Bt., Retired Soldier and Country Stockbroker.

"Sorry to disturb you, doctor, but could you come at once, please. The baby has swallowed the corkscrew."

Five minutes later, just as he has got dressed, another call:

"Oh, I'm so glad I've caught you. Sorry to have disturbed you, but everything is all right now — we've found another corkscrew."

Air Chief Marshal Sir Robert Freer, G.B.E., K.C.B., Commandant, Royal College of Defence Studies.

The bishop, who was a keen DIY man, was watching a carpenter at work in the house and trying to pick up the odd tip. But the young carpenter found it a little off-putting and shortly hit his finger with the hammer, whereupon he let out a cry of "bloody hell!".

The bishop tut-tutted and remonstrated, saying he should count to ten and pray for easement.

Unconvinced but chastened, the carpenter continued growing all the more nervous at the bishop's presence. Sure enough disaster struck again, the chisel slicing off the end of his thumb. Stifling a scream he looked at the bishop, gritted his teeth and prayed. Whereupon the piece of thumb suddenly leapt back into place.

"Jesus Christ," said the carpenter.

"Bloody hell," said the bishop.

Major-General John Dutton Frost, C.B., D.S.O. and Bar, M.C., (Retired), Now Farming in West Sussex.

Soon after the end of the war, the senior officers of the Commandos and the Parachute Regiment lunched together at Aldershot. Afterwards, we were all lined up outside for a photograph. Among those present were Admiral of the Fleet Lord Mountbatten and Field Marshal Lord Montgomery.

When it seemed we were all ready, the Field Marshal asked the photographer, a brash young man, how he thought we looked. The man replied:

"Speaking frankly, I think you look quite horrible."

Monty leapt to his feet, turned round to us and said:

"Do you think he means all of us, or just me?"

Professor Dennis Butler Fry,
Professor of Experimental Phonetics, University College London, 1958–75.

Many stories are told of the absent-mindedness and the depths of professorial abstraction achieved by the late Professor Norbert Wiener, who was a mathematical prodigy and among other things, the inventor, so to speak, of the science of cybernetics, for which he coined the name.

One of the most often repeated stories tells of the occasion when he and his family were to move to a new apartment. His wife was well aware of his tendencies, so when he left in the morning for the day's work, she handed him a piece of paper and a key, saying:

"Now, Norbert, we're moving today: here is the address of the new apartment on this piece of paper and here is the key. So remember, don't come back here tonight, go to the new apartment," and she put the key and the piece of paper in his pocket.

In the course of the day someone asked him a question requiring a fairly abstruse mathematical answer, so he took the piece of paper out of his pocket and wrote the necessary equation on the back of it. The young man who had asked the question said:

"Yes, I think I see, Professor, but do you mind if I keep this paper?"

"Go ahead," said Professor Wiener, and thought no more of the matter.

At the end of the day he went, of course, to the old apartment, and it was only when he tried the key and found that it did not open the door that he remembered he should have gone to the new apartment. But where was it? The paper with the address had mysteriously disappeared. So the professor went down again to the street and stopped the first personable looking lad he saw, saying:

"Say, I'm Norbert Wiener. You wouldn't happen to know where I live, would you?"

"Why sure, dad. Mom knew you'd be here and sent me to fetch you," said the boy.

Air Vice-Marshal Jack Furner, C.B.E., D.F.C., A.F.C., (Retired),
Assistant Air Secretary, Ministry of Defence, 1973–76.

An Indian village was having trouble with a marauding tiger. The Elders of the village decided to call in a reputable tiger catcher. He was experienced in his trade and spent many days searching out the tracks of the approaching tiger and eventually decided upon a look-out position in the branches of a strategically placed tree. He waited in the branches for nights on end with his gun at the ready and, at last one night his vigilance was rewarded when he heard the approaching tiger rustling through the undergrowth.

His training was such as to make him wait until he could see the whites of the tiger's eyes and, at what he judged to be the appropriate moment, he fired — confidently — just once — right between the eyes. His search in the morning revealed no tiger. This whole sequence was repeated twice more. On the fourth occasion he decided to take a torch along. And at the right time he flashed the torch. There, lit up by the beam, were two tigers with their off-side eyes shut.

Extract from an officer's Annual Confidential Appraisal Report:
"Men will follow this officer — if only out of sheer curiosity."

The Pope, the Archbishop of Canterbury and the Moderator of the Church of Scotland were enjoying a day together fishing in a little dinghy on a beautiful lake. They made an early start at dawn and around about eight o'clock in the morning, feeling a little peckish, they decided that somebody ought to go back for their packed breakfasts.

The Pope offered to go back to the shore, stepped out of the boat, walked across the water, came back with the breakfasts and they went on fishing through the sunlit morning.

At about midday, the Archbishop volunteered to collect lunch, stepped out of the boat, walked across the water and came back with packed lunches. The sultry afternoon wore on and four o'clock approached.

The Moderator volunteered to go back for tea, stepped out of the boat and went 'kaplonk' into the water. The Pope nudged the Archbishop:

"Do you suppose we should have told him about those stepping stones?"

An eastern potentate had before him a peasant convicted of a serious felony. The traditional penalty was death. However, he was an enlightened potentate and always gave the convicted in these cases a choice before death. He told the peasant:

"You may make one last statement. If that statement is true you will be hanged and if it is false you will be beheaded." The peasant was no fool. He hardly hesitated before making his statement:

"I shall be beheaded."

**Air Vice-Marshal Maxwell Gardham, C.B., C.B.E.,
Registrar, Ashridge College, Berkhamsted.**

The bishop had received quite a few letters about a certain young curé who, in the opinion of the writers, had far too beautiful and attractive a housekeeper. The bishop decided to pay a visit to the parish and went to stay with the curé. There was no doubt that the housekeeper was both young and very beautiful, but all seemed to be in perfect order and the bishop could find no fault at all in the way in which the young curé behaved towards her. The bishop was taken on a conducted tour of the parish and was shown the highly prized candlesticks of solid gold which stood on the altar in the village church.

The bishop took his leave. Three days later he received a letter from the curé telling of the odd fact that the candlesticks had been found to be missing. The curé wrote:

"Of course, I do not say that a man so eminent as Your Grace has taken the candlesticks, but I think you must agree that the disappearance of the candlesticks on the day of Your Grace's departure could be taken as strong circumstantial evidence."

The bishop replied:

"My son, I do not accuse you of sleeping with your housekeeper, but you must agree that the circumstantial evidence is very strong. You see, had you slept in your own bed after my departure you would have found those candlesticks!"

A flea went into a bar and ordered a double scotch. He knocked it back and ordered another, and another, and yet another. Then he hopped unsteadily out onto the pavement, leapt high in the air and fell flat on his face.

"Dammit," he said, "someone's moved my dog!"

Sir Peter Garran, K.C.M.G.,
Formerly H.M. Ambassador to the Netherlands.

Three American college girls, one from Wellesley, one from Vassar and one from Smith, were one day discussing the question, if they should be wrecked on a desert island, what kind of man would they wish to share their lot?

The girl from Wellesley said that if that was what fate had in store for her she would of course want him to be tall, dark, handsome and passionate.

The girl from Vassar said she would indeed want a man well versed in the arts of love, but there was more to life than that. In between, he must also be able to talk intelligently about literature, poetry, art and music.

But the girl from Smith said simply:

"Well, I guess I'd settle for a really competent obstetrician."

Professor Stephen Denis Garrett, F.R.S.,
Emeritus Professor of Mycology, University of Cambridge.

A bishop, addressing a school for small boys, remarked:

"I can remember a dormitory with seven little boys in it. When the lights were turned out, six boys stayed in bed but the seventh got out, knelt down and said his prayers. Can you think of anything braver than that?"

Boy: "Yes, sir, I can."

Bishop (somewhat startled): "Well, my little man, what is it?"

Boy: "Well, sir, I can think of a dormitory with seven bishops in it. When the lights were turned out, six bishops got out of bed, knelt down and said their prayers, but the seventh bishop stayed in bed."

Major-General James M.L. Gavin, C.B., C.B.E.,
Director, British Standards Institution.

Little girl, taken to the ballet for the first time and fascinated by the dancers on the tips of their toes:

"Mummy, why don't they get taller ladies?"

The little boy's puppy was sick and his mother said:

"We must take him to the vet — that's an animal doctor."

The little boy thought for some time, then:

"Mummy," he said, "will this animal doctor be a dog or a cat?"

Peter W. Gibbings,
Chairman of The Guardian and Manchester Evening News Ltd.

A definition given by Archbishop Coggan:
Hospitality is the art of making people *feel* at home when you wish they *were* at home.

Air Marshal Sir Gerald Gibbs, K.B.E., C.I.E., M.C.,
Senior Air Staff Officer, No. 11 Group, Fighter Command in Battle of Britain, 1940.

A man was out on a lonely country walk one day when he looked at his watch and discovered that it had stopped. This worried him because he didn't want to be late home — and then fortunately he spotted a man milking a cow.

So he went up to him and asked him if he could tell him the right time.

"Yes, 'deed I can zur," said the man, "and right to a few minutes." He sat down again on the milking stool, pressed the cow's udder and looked carefully.

"Quarter past three, zur," he said.

"I am so grateful," said the walker, "and I do think it is wonderful the way you people who live deep in the country can judge things by physical phenomena. I suppose you are able to tell the time by the pressure of the cow's udder, your knowledge of when she was last milked, and so on."

"No, zur, not quite like that, zur," said the man. "It's like this. I git down on me stool and I presses her udder gentle — like this. I then looks careful — and I can see church clock!"

Field Marshal Sir Roland Gibbs, G.C.B., C.B.E., D.S.O., M.C., Chief of the General Staff, 1976–79.

An irascible senior officer in a military hospital was boring the staff with his grumbles. It came to a head one day when he finished a long list of complaints by saying to the sister:

"And what's more, young woman, why can't you do something about the bed-pans? The design of the thing hasn't changed since Waterloo."

"No," replied the sister, "and what's more, neither has the shape of the human bottom."

Rear-Admiral Philip D. Gick, C.B., O.B.E., D.S.C. and Bar, Fleet Air Arm Pilot until 1964; now Chairman of Emsworth Shipyard.

During the war, whilst a lieutenant in the Navy, I was asked by my father, on a day when I was passing through London, to lunch with him at a meeting of the Anchorites. He was then chairman and the guest of honour was A. V. Alexander, then First Lord of the Admiralty. I was introduced to an elderly Roman Catholic priest, Canon Hanney, whom I knew as the author of many delightful stories written under the name of George A. Birmingham. Throughout the lunch he entertained me delightfully and just before the First Lord started to speak, he said to me:

"You are about to hear a wonderful example of the art of public speaking. Throughout his speech Mr. Alexander will be cheered and applauded and will probably be given a standing ovation at the end. Take this pencil and every time he says something you have not heard often before, or which is not a well-known platitude, just make a mark on the tablecloth."

The speech went precisely as planned and when we sat down, Canon Hanney pointed to the clean tablecloth:

"You see, my boy, it matters not what you say, but how you say it."

Sir John Gielgud, C.H., Actor and Director.

A youngster was appearing in a small part with Mrs. Patrick Campbell, the great Edwardian actress. His character's name in the play was Colonel

Ponting. At one performance he was trying to inject some life into the role, only to be rewarded by Mrs. Campbell remarking in a loud aside:

"Oh, somewhat Colonel Disappointing tonight."

Major-General John Galbraith Gill, C.B.E., D.S.O., M.C., Late R.A.M.C.

A South Wales chapel had outside a notice board which said on it:

"Where will you be on Judgement Day?"

Underneath this someone had written:

"Waiting for the Cardiff bus."

At a village wedding the vicar gave out the final hymn:

"Hymn number 540." There was no response from the organist who had turned round towards the vicar and shook his head at him.

The vicar, knowing something was amiss, looked at his sheet.

"Sorry," he said, "hymn number 520. 'Love divine, all loves excelling'."

Hymn number 540 was 'Fight the good fight with all thy might'.

From Castle Acre Magazine, Norfolk.

Dear Head Teacher, Robert has swallowed a 50 pence piece. I am keeping him in bed but will be calling in the doctor if there is no change by Monday.

Professor Iain E. Gillespie, M.D., F.R.C.S., Professor of Surgery, University of Manchester, since 1970.

We reveal our national characteristics in the small incidents in daily life; for example the response to a request for another lump of sugar in a cup of tea. In England this is a most civilised experience with a Georgian silver sugar-bowl (plus tongs), being offered on a fine silver salver with a delicate Nottingham lace mat.

In Ireland the brown paper sugar bag will be shoved along the bare table to you.

In Scotland, your hostess will smile thinly, and say:

"But are you sure you've stirred the first lump properly?"

In January the landlord of a pub in Aberdeen put out a large gallon whisky bottle to collect donations for a local worthy charity. Just before Christmas it was stolen, but the police said they were confident of an early arrest, as both coins had been marked.

Lord Gisborough, D.L.,
Landowner and Farmer.

A ship was lying off a foreign port and the mate came back aboard from a visit ashore dead drunk. So the captain wrote in the log that the mate was drunk. The latter was furious but the captain explained and the mate had to admit that he had been so, and that the entry was absolutely factual.

The mate asked the captain if it was, therefore, all right to enter any remarks in the log when he was on duty, provided they were absolutely true, and the captain, of course, agreed.

Next day, the captain went ashore and checked the log the following morning as he was accustomed to do. The mate had written:

"Today the captain was sober!"

Lord Glenamara, P.C., C.H.,
Leader, House of Commons, 1974–76; Chairman, Cable and Wireless, since 1976.

Two men at the cinema were watching the huge figure of John Wayne approach the low door of a Mexican taverna.

"Bet you a pound he bangs his head," said the first man.

"O.K. — you're on," replied the second man.

Sure enough he did bang his head, whereupon the first man said:

"I've got to be honest — I've seen the film before."

"So have I," replied the second man, "but I didn't think he'd do it a second time."

Lord Glentoran, K.B.E.,
Formerly Speaker of Senate, Northern Ireland.

An English tourist in the west of Ireland stopped to ask a local the way to Dublin. The reply he received was:

"If I was going to Dublin I wouldn't start from here."

Sir Colin Goad, K.C.M.G.,
Secretary-General, Inter-Governmental Maritime Consultative Organisation, 1968–73.

During the Congress of Vienna, Prince Metternich, the Austrian Chancellor, was rudely awakened by his valet de chambre during the night.
"Sir, sir," said the valet, "the Russian Ambassador has died in his sleep."
Metternich pondered awhile and uttered:
"I wonder what his motive was for doing that?"

Sir Ernest Goodale, C.B.E., M.C.,
Formerly President, Silk and Rayon Users' Association.

Advice from an experienced after-dinner speaker to a young aspirant:
"If you haven't struck oil in the first five minutes, stop boring!"

Professor Albert Goodwin,
Emeritus Professor of Modern History, University of Manchester.

One of the stories which used to circulate in the Jesus College Senior Common Room and which has since attained a somewhat wider audience, concerns a former and long-dead colleague, E.E. Genner, Senior Tutor and a strict Nonconformist and uncompromising teetotaller. After being passed over for the post of Principal, he had created a precedent in the university by transferring himself, in high dudgeon, to Oriel College as Tutor for Honour Moderations. At his first appearance in the Oriel S.C.R. he was placed next to the Provost — Phelps — who courteously, but somewhat incautiously, invited him to take a glass of port at dessert. Genner, bristling at what he regarded as an affront to his strongly held principles, replied:
"Rather than do that, I would commit adultery."
"But," said the Provost, declining rather than accepting the challenge, "who wouldn't?"

The Late Lord Goronwy-Roberts,
Deputy Leader of the Opposition, House of Lords, 1975–79.

When he returned from the Congress of Berlin, Disraeli admitted to Lord Salisbury that it had been a bit of a strain, particularly when Bismarck took him into his room and heavily recounted one 'risible anecdote' after another.

"And you know, my dear Salisbury, a German joke is no laughing matter."

Sir Ronald Gould,
Formerly General Secretary, National Union of Teachers.

An Irish priest trying to console a woman who had just lost her father, asked her:

"And what would have been your father's last words?"

She replied:

"Me father had no last words. Mother was with him till the end."

A cricket enthusiast had three trays installed in his office labelled 'In', 'Out' and 'L.B.W.'.

A visitor remarked he could see the significance of 'In' and 'Out' but what did 'L.B.W.' mean?

And the cricket enthusiast replied:

"Let the b——s wait."

General Sir Ian Gourlay, K.C.B., O.B.E., M.C.,
Commandant-General, Royal Marines, 1971–75.

When Sir Francis Chichester was expected back in Plymouth after his epic trip round the world single-handed, special preparations were put in hand for his reception in the Sound. To certain young Royal Marines fell the task of providing a close escort of rubber landing craft for his yacht. Appreciating the TV opportunities for publicity which the occasion would afford, they took great care to see that 'ROYAL MARINES' was painted prominently on the hull of their craft.

A member of the Parachute Brigade, with whom the Marines have always had a lively rivalry, was watching the painting of the boats and ventured to ask whether the Marines had considered what sort of publicity they would achieve if their craft turned over in full view of the TV audiences of the world.

"Certainly," they replied, "we have painted on the bottom... 'PARACHUTE BRIGADE'!"

When Mr. Edward Heath was Prime Minister he happened one day to be in Belfast visiting the security forces and chose to call in on a Royal Marine Commando unit. It is commonly accepted that a soldier's lot in Northern Ireland is a demanding one. The work can be dangerous, the hours long and the living conditions trying.

Mr. Heath must have been well aware of all this when he went up to a Marine on watch in a particularly difficult area and said to him:

"Well! Tell me, what are your problems?"

The young Marine, just eighteen and very conscious of the expectancy with which everyone round was waiting upon his reply, proved equal to the moment. Looking his Prime Minister straight in the face he said proudly:

"Problems are not my department, sir!"

The United World Colleges were holding an international council meeting presided over by Lord Mountbatten. The representative from Iran, a lady, was explaining how she had recently been involved with a certain educational committee and had become its chairman. Correcting herself hastily she went on, while showing a fine grasp of a fashionable colloquialism of the day:

"Perhaps I should more properly say I was a chairperson!"

This was pretty quick for an on-the-spur-of-the-moment comment, but not as quick as Lord Mountbatten's lightning rejoinder from the chair:

"NOT chairperson," he interjected to the delight of all present, "you mean chair-PERSIAN!"

Professor Brian G. Gowenlock,
Professor of Chemistry, Heriot-Watt University, Edinburgh.

The angel guarding the gates of heaven answered to a knock at the door. There was a man asking if he could come in.

"You are welcome," said the angel, "but I would like to know whether you have performed any courageous act in your life. Without it you cannot enter."

The man said:

"Well, in fact I can. You see," he went on, "though I am by profession an accountant, my hobby is being a rugby referee."

"Indeed," said the angel, "and were there opportunities for courageous acts as a referee?"

"Yes," said the man. "I was refereeing an International at Cardiff Arms Park when Wales were playing Scotland. Wales were winning by three points and the game had gone into injury time. One of the Scottish players kicked ahead from his own 22 and in the move that followed he finally went over by the corner flag, though the crowd all claimed that he had stepped into touch carrying the ball. Nevertheless, I awarded the try and Scotland won."

"Well," said the angel, "that was indeed a courageous act, provided of course that it can be verified."

He pressed a button and spoke on his celestial telephone to the Records and Computing Department and asked them to check the story. Before long, the phone rang and having listened to the message the angel said to the would-be entrant:

"It appears that our Records Department is unable to verify your story — no such records exist. Can you tell me when this happened?"

The man looked at his watch and said:

"Yes, as a matter of fact it was about five minutes ago."

**Major-General Ferris Nelson Grant, C.B.,
Commander, Plymouth Group, Royal Marines, 1965–68.**

The bishop was visiting a remote parish church for a confirmation service. On arrival he was met by the vicar and a young man. The latter asked to carry his bag and the bishop said:

"Thank you, you will find my kit in the boot of the car."

When he was robed and arrived at the altar he found laid out, all cleaned, his jack, two spanners, a hammer and wheel brace.

(True story from Bishop Westall.)

James Shaw Grant, C.B.E., LL.D.,
Chairman, Pitlochry Festival Theatre.

I am very cynical about official letters of commendation. With good reason. When the *Stornoway Gazette* celebrated its Golden Jubilee, the managing director invited prominent Lewismen to write short messages for a feature page. Best known among them was Iain Macleod, then Shadow Chancellor of the Exchequer. To maintain a political balance he sent a similar invitation to the Prime Minister. My wife was very amused. She could discover no discernible link between Harold Wilson and the *Stornoway Gazette*.

"I hope they've invited General de Gaulle," she commented. "I would love to see a message 'Vive la Gazette'."

Shortly after the invitations went out, I had to visit St. Andrew's House as Chairman of the Crofters' Commission. I was introduced to a member of the information staff I had not met before.

"Ah," he said, "you should be able to help me. You're bound to know something about the *Stornoway Gazette*." He had no idea that I had been editor of the *Gazette* for thirty years and was still the major shareholder. With great goodwill I gave him the help he wanted — drafting a letter of commendation from the Prime Minister to my own newspaper.

Sir Arthur Grattan-Bellew, C.M.G., Q.C.,
Formally a Legal Adviser at the Foreign and Commonwealth Office.

When I was at the Bar many years ago, a story was told about a famous judge. I believe it was true, but I can't be sure.

Mr. Justice Pollock frequently heard cases in which expert witnesses gave evidence, and his brother, Freddie, a consulting engineer, frequently gave expert evidence. At some social function, someone asked the judge to define the expression 'expert witness'. The judge thought for a moment and then said:

"There are three categories of expert witnesses — liars, bloody liars, and my brother Freddie."

84

Lord Greenhill of Harrow, G.C.M.G., O.B.E., Former Head of Diplomatic Service.

Judge (confronting prisoner in dock): "Who is going to defend you?"
Prisoner: "I need no man to defend me. The Lord is my defender."
Judge: "You would be well advised to employ someone better known locally."

Lord Greenwood of Rossendale, P.C., J.P., D.L., LL.D., Politician.

One year the National Federation of Fish Fryers were holding their annual conference at the same time that the National Union of Journalists were holding theirs. The Federation sent the following telegram to the N.U.J.:
"Fraternal greetings. Our work is wrapped up in yours."

Joseph Greig, Actor.

I believe that this is a true story:

Mrs. Sinclair, an 80-year-old widow, lived in Sandwick in the Shetland Isles. She was visiting her dentist to have her dentures renewed and while in his waiting room read in an old magazine an article on cremation. Next time she visited her doctor she brought up the subject.

"Dr. Robertson, I have been reading about this cremation and I think it is a splendid idea. Do you think I could arrange to have it done in my Will?"

The doctor explained that as there were no facilities at that time in Shetland the cremation would have to be carried out in Aberdeen. Mrs. Sinclair thought for a moment, then said:

"In that case I won't bother, as I get so sick on the boat."

Sir Francis Griffin,
Leader, Birmingham City Council, 1964–72.

The councillor had worked hard to get the family rehoused and called to see how they liked their new house. The small son was sitting on the doorstep.

"Well, Tommy, how do you like your new home. No more over-crowding, eh?"

"Well, no," said Tommy, "I have me own room, me sister has hers, but poor old mum still has to sleep with dad."

John Selwyn Gummer, M.P.,
Member of Parliament for Eye, Suffolk.

The Llanelli rugby team came up to London to play the Barbarians, but at the last minute they found they had only got fourteen men. The captain of the Barbarians — a perfect English gentleman with the rounded vowels of the better public school — came up to the Welsh captain and said:

"I hear you're one man short, old chap; we would be very happy to lend you one of our reserves."

The Welsh captain replied easily:

"Oh no, boyo, no need; we don't intend to be one man down too long."

Sir John Gutch, K.C.M.G., O.B.E.,
Formerly High Commissioner for the Western Pacific.

When I was High Commissioner for the Western Pacific in the late fifties, my wife was anxious to form a company of Girl Guides in Honiara in the Solomon Islands. Brownies were already established there, but it was difficult to obtain recruits of the age to become Guides, as parents were suspicious of any innovations involving their daughters. It was therefore decided, with the co-operation of the Matron at the Honiara hospital, to form the new company from the girls in training as nurses.

All went well. New uniforms arrived for the Guides and were worn with great pride. After some months, however, it was noticed that some of the girls' uniforms were less well fitting than before and it fell to the Matron to take the girls concerned to task for the serious lapse in their moral behaviour which had evidently occurred.

In the course of her remarks she referred to the girls' membership of the Guides and the disgrace which they had brought on the uniforms which they had been so proud to wear. The girls concerned looked injured and protested:

"But Matron, we weren't wearing our uniforms at the time!"

The Earl of Haddington, K.T., M.C., T.D., F.R.S.E., F.S.A. Scot., LL.D., Author; Trustee, National Library of Scotland.

A certain parish minister asked my father for permission to fish the Eden Water at Mellerstain. This was duly granted for a specific day, but on the next day and on others following, the factor noticed the minister again on the river bank, and expostulated with him.

Factor: "Lord Binning told me that he had allowed you just a day's fishing."

Minister: "Ah, but remember! The word of the Lord endureth forever."

A constable on his beat meets a belated reveller, hirpling along with one foot on the pavement, and the other in the gutter.

Reveller: "Hullo! Whatever is the matter with me?"

Constable: "You are drunk, sir, that's what is the matter with you."

Reveller: "Thank heavens! I thought I was lame!"

Archibald Richard Burdon Haldane, C.B.E., Writer to the Signet; Late Trustee, National Library of Scotland.

A strict Scottish minister of the Church had married a young and attractive wife with a taste for nice frocks. On one occasion the wife went off to Glasgow for the day, returning with a large cardboard box. On being questioned by her husband she confessed that she had bought an expensive new frock. The husband taxed his wife with having spent so much on mere finery.

"Yes," replied the wife, "I'm afraid the devil tempted me."

"Did you not say to the tempter, 'get ye behind me'?" said the husband.

"Yes, John," replied his wife, "I did, but all he said was: 'It looks even nicer from behind'."

An Elder of the Church of Scotland, much given to strong language, at last consulted the minister as to a remedy. The latter advised him to put a pebble in his pocket each time he swore and to bring the pebbles to church on the following Sunday. When Sunday came the Elder handed to the minister a handful of pebbles, explaining that these were for the 'Blasts'. On the minister remarking that this was not too bad, the Elder added:

"Bide a wee, meenister, there's a cairt coming up the hill wi' the 'Damns'."

Sir Douglas Hall, Bt., K.C.M.G., J.P., Last Governor of the Somaliland Protectorate.

It was April 1931. I had been in the Colonial Administrative Service for something under a year and was stationed at Kalomo in the Batoka (later Southern) Province of what was then Northern Rhodesia. There was a famine in the Zambezi valley, and relief was being organised from a camp about halfway down the escarpment, able-bodied men being employed in making a motor road into the area in return for enough maize for their often large families. Although this is not part of the story it is pleasant to report that no lives were lost. The scheme organised by my District Commissioner worked well.

Sam Facey was in charge of the camp. He was a District Officer of three or four years' experience, which, to me, meant he was a man of vast experience, but he had been at the camp for some time and the District Commissioner sent me to relieve him.

I could not speak the local language, Chitonga. Rightly or wrongly, I had decided to get my lower standard language examination out of the way when I found that the Chinyanja I had been taught during the Colonial

Service Course at Oxford had taken me to a point not too far away from a pass standard. But there was an African at the camp, Siamunthu, who was fluent in Chinyanja and so would be able to interpret for me. The fact that he knew no English would be good for my studies.

I arrived at the camp, learned the routine from Sam, and saw him off in the lorry which had brought me. He mentioned that I was lucky to be in such a good game area. Good from the point of view of both animals and birds.

When the last ration had been issued for the day, Siamunthu suggested we should go out shooting.

"Good," I said. "What shall we go for?"

"Lions," he replied.

I must say my spirits fell sharply.

"All right," I said, hoping I did not look as frightened as I felt. "I'll get my rifle and we'll set off." I was a little depressed to note that he carried only an ancient muzzle loader.

"You'd be much better off with a shot-gun," commented Siamunthu. "No. 5 shot would be about right."

Worse and worse. If I must use a shot-gun, at least I might have been allowed to use cartridges that carried heavy shot. I had a box of S.S.G. in my tent, but I was too shy to go against Siamunthu's advice.

"Mr. Facey used to go after lions every evening," remarked Siamunthu in a conversational way.

"Oh!" I said, and feeling that something was expected from me to keep the conversation alive I added:

"How many used he to shoot each time?"

"It depended on how many there were about," said Siamunthu. "Sometimes he just shot two or three. Sometimes only one. On one occasion when we were very lucky he shot six."

I was wishing most heartily that I was back in the safety of the little District Office at Kalomo. Why was it that I had ever found things a little boring there?

"Mr. Facey was very fond of lions," went on Siamunthu. "There was nothing he liked better than roast lion for supper. Often he enjoyed a fried leg for breakfast, and if he was going to be away from the camp for the middle of the day, he would probably take another cold leg for lunch."

I knew that Sam was well built, and quite a chap one way and another.

No doubt a diet of approximately one lion per day had something to do with this. But it didn't make me feel any happier.

A few minutes later Siamunthu remarked that we should probably see the lions quite soon. I hoped that the shaking of my legs, so obvious to me, was not equally obvious to him. What a lovely place that little office at Kalomo was. How happy I had been struggling with the station accounts there.

"There they are!" whispered Siamunthu, hoarsely, his mouth right up to my ear. "Dozens and dozens of them!" he added excitedly. "What a bit of luck!"

By now I was nearly blind with fear, but not so blind that I did not see a flock of guinea fowl get up in front of me. I was never able to explain to Siamunthu why I did not even raise my gun, let alone try a right and left. After all, it would have been a bit stupid to point out that fear drained away all strength from my arms.

An hour or two later, relaxing in a deck chair in front of the camp fire, and vowing to myself that no one would ever know what had happened, I thought how stupid it was that the Chinyanja word for lion should be 'mkango' and for guinea fowl 'nkhanga'. After all, when you are not yet even quite at lower standard level, there is precious little difference between the two.

Sir John B. Hall, Bt.,
Merchant Banker.

Customer, waiting for appointment in hall of large city bank, to uniformed commissionaire:

"How many people work here?"

Commissionaire (an old soldier): "About half of them, sir."

An Englishman in Paris hails a taxi, explaining he is late for a train from the Gare d'Austerlitz. The driver does his best, but reaches the station two minutes after the train's departure time. Sadly he turns to his fare and says:

"Hélas, monsieur, ce n'est pas Austerlitz — c'est Waterloo!"

Captain Sir Robert Stirling-Hamilton, Bt., J.P., D.L., R.N.

In Festival of Britain year I was bidden to a large and formal dinner at Holyrood, given by the High Commissioner for Scotland. This was one of a series and the guests that evening were mostly from the Church and the Royal Navy.

After a splendid meal, a somewhat long-winded gentleman rose to propose a toast to the Church. I am sure that he expressed all the right sentiments and it was not his fault if some of his audience let their attention wander a little before he finally lifted his glass and gave us:

"The Kirk o' Scotland."

As the guests repeated this, the loudest voice came from a distinguished R.N. captain with:

"The Curse of Scotland!"

The clerics laughed as much as the others, while the captain was busy trying to cover up by saying that he just thought that this strange toast was an old Scottish custom.

The Late Lord Hamnett, D.L., J.P.,
Chairman, Warrington New Town Development Corporation, 1969–77.

Two men, father and son, were stood together on the beach of a forgotten Pacific island, which was still notorious for indulging in occasional cannibalism. They were watching the flotsam from what had obviously been a wrecked ship at sea, when there came stumbling ashore a very beautiful blonde, scantily clothed after her immersion in the waves.

The son turned to the father, saying:

"Say, dad, shall I rush into the water, bring her ashore, take her home and we'll eat her?"

The father, full of contemplative wisdom, looked at the vision rising from the waves and replied:

"No, son, rush into the water, bring her ashore, take her home and we'll eat your mother."

There once was a company secretary who, having to make a speech at the end of the annual meeting where he was expected to pay tribute to the staff for the past year's efforts and loyalty, concluded by turning to his secretary, putting his hand familiarly on her shoulder and saying:

"And now there's Clarissa,
Quite the nicest of the bunch,
But down in the accounts,
She's petrol, oil and lunch."

Sir Charles Hardie, C.B.E., Chartered Accountant.

A balloonist told me recently that, despite all modern contrivances, such as altimeters and radar, when a balloon is in a cloud it is impossible to find out in which direction you are going. What you do, therefore, is take a piece of ordinary tissue and throw it over the side of the basket — if it goes down, you know you are going up, and you DEFLATE — if it goes up, you know you are going down, and you INFLATE.

I would swear that as I was passing 11 Downing Street one recent weekend, just before the season of Budget decisions, I saw the Chancellor of the Exchequer, leaning out of the bathroom window at the side — doing, what do you think? — throwing out little pieces of tissue.

Lord Harmar-Nicholls, J.P., Businessman; Member Euro-Parliament.

Chinese soldier to British Tommy: "When you British go to war you always seem to win, but when we go to war we always seem to lose, why is that?"

British Tommy: "That's easy. Before we British go to battle we always pray."

Chinese soldier: "It can't be that, because before we go to battle we too always pray."

British Tommy: "Yes, but who the hell can understand Chinese!"

Rex Harris,
Author and Broadcaster.

An example of The Savage Club's impromptu wit:

The Club having left Carlton House Terrace due to expiration of lease, moved from pillar to post until suitable premises were found in King Street, Covent Garden.

After some months of renovations and decorations the opening day was watched by the neighbouring porters. One approached a member as he was entering and asked:

"Excuse me, guv, but is this a gentleman's club or can anybody join?"

The member shook his head sorrowfully and said:

"I am sorry to say that the answer to both your questions is in the negative."

Martin Richard Harris,
Deputy Chairman, Reckitt & Colman Ltd.

President Lyndon Johnson, of the United States, when introduced in over-flattering terms, is reputed to have said:

"I do so wish that my parents could have been present today. My father would have liked what was said about me; my mother would have believed it."

Sir Frank Hartley, C.B.E., D.Sc., F.R.S.C., F.P.S.,
Recently Vice-Chancellor, University of London; Vice-Chairman, Medicines Commission.

An old lady, having enjoyed two sermons by a new young curate who had just joined her parish church, said to him, to the surprise of all who heard:

"I think you're wonderful. I never really knew what sin meant until you came."

Macdonald Hastings,
Author; Editor and Journalist.

With due solemnity, for two hundred years, the vintage port after dinner has been passed clockwise round the table. It is a tradition which has persisted, with only regrettable lapses, up to the present time.

It is told of an English country squire who had, as such men do, raised a large family of children that in his old age, his children grown up, he carried on a lifelong custom. Every morning his butler, with the aid of a candle and a subtle hand in pulling the cork, released the nectar into a Waterford decanter, making sure that none of the sediment leaked into the glass.

In childhood his children put up with the ceremony. In the mischief of adolescence they decided one day to call father's bluff. They poured the nectar from his decanter into the rose garden and replaced it with something they had collected for a few shillings from the local grocer.

After dinner they watched wide-eyed as the old man settled again into his port. Nosing it, he said:

"Magnificent!"

Bursting their sides, the children revealed where they had bought it. The old man pressed the bell for his butler.

"How long have you worked for me, James?"

"Thirty-one years, sir."

"You're sacked. You have been selling my Taylor's 1927 to the village grocer."

Sir Claude Hayes, K.C.M.G.,
Former Chairman, Crown Agents.

The builder who repaired my house had the contract for Chartwell. He told me that one day soon after the last war his men were putting in a fire escape from a top room, of the kind in which a chair descends slowly on a rope, adjusting its speed to the weight of the escaper. Along came Sir Winston, and of course he insisted on trying it, brushing aside warnings that it had not been tested. He did; it let him slowly down the front of the house, and stopped halfway. There he hung, spinning first one way and then the other.

It was half an hour before he could be lowered to the ground, and the builder and his men ever since have considered his uninterrupted address to them at least as inspiring as any of his wartime speeches.

Vice-Admiral Sir John Hayes, K.C.B., O.B.E.,
Lord-Lieutenant of Ross and Cromarty, Skye and Lochalsh, since 1977.

As a captain in the late 'fifties I was privileged to command H.M.S. *St. Vincent*, a naval training establishment in Gosport for eight hundred boys aged sixteen who spent a year in this 'stone frigate' prior to joining the Fleet as Junior Seamen. They were of all shapes and sizes.

The daily parade on weekdays was taken by me. On Sundays, a visiting admiral from the Portsmouth Command or from sea added lustre to the ceremonial inspection and march-past led by the bugle band. This was followed, in those days, by compulsory church.

In vain did I often suggest to my distinguished guest, who may not have always been so familiar with the repartee of the young sailor, that the smaller the frame the brighter he was likely to be; for there is a temptation always to single out the smallest in the middle of the front rank for such questioning and which invariably received the riposte it deserved.

On this occasion the impressively tall admiral in sword and medals stopped before five-foot-nothing, rigidly at attention.

"And what, my lad, did you have for breakfast this morning?"

"Bacon and eggs, sir."

"How often does your mother give you that at home?"

"Never, sir."

"Well, that's one good reason for joining the Navy, isn't it?"
"I *hate* bacon and eggs, sir."

Air Marshal Sir Maurice Heath, K.B.E., C.B., C.V.O., D.L., Extra Gentleman Usher to the Queen; Member of Council, Officers' Pension Society.

In December 1929 Pilot Officer Heath was posted from No. 16 Squadron at Old Sarum, Wiltshire, to No. 28 Squadron, Ambala, India, on a five-year overseas tour. Travelling out by the troopship H.M.T. *Somersetshire*, he met on board two other young officers destined for the same squadron — Flying Officers L.V.G. Barrow and L.F. Sinclair (now Air Vice-Marshal Sir Laurence Sinclair).

On disembarkation in India the three officers discovered that the train which was to take them to Ambala did not arrive there until the somewhat ungodly hour of 0200 on the morning of the third day. Unaware at that time that because Ambala lay midway between the two important cities of Delhi and Lahore this was the normal arrival and departure time for Ambala, Heath suggested they had better send a telegram to the C.O. of No. 28 Squadron informing him of their date and time of arrival. This was agreed and the telegram dispatched. The three young officers were also, at this time, unaware of the vagaries of the Indian Telegraph Service, which even in those days was staffed exclusively by Indian clerks.

At 0200 hours precisely three days later the train steamed into Ambala station and the three newest members of the squadron tumbled out to be met by the Adjutant wearing mess uniform and a greatcoat and accompanied by four officers of flight lieutenant rank. The Adjutant, one Flight Lieutenant Berryman, approached and said sternly:

"Heath, Barrow and Sinclair?"

"Yes, sir," they replied.

"And which of you jokers thought to pull your new Commanding Officer's leg by sending this telegram?" he asked.

"I d-did, sir," stammered Heath. "We thought it was such a dreadful time to arrive that we should let him know."

Berryman held out the telegram. It read:

"Arriving Ambala 0200 hours, 22nd December, signed Heart Brocken and Sincere."

Sir John Hedges, C.B.E.,
Former Chairman, Berkshire Area Health Authority.

In the late 19th century my father lived in a Berkshire village where people did not use the expression 'D.V.', but said, 'if spared'.

One day a new widow went to see the rector and said:

"I'm sorry to tell you, rector, that my husband has passed away and wishes to be buried Thursday, if spared."

Brigadier Sir Mark Henniker, Bt., C.B.E., D.S.O., M.C., D.L.,
Retired Army Officer.

In the North African Campaign of 1942–43 the American military practice of building camp latrines as 10-seater affairs, with no partitions or doors, became universal in both Allied armies. Nonetheless, it took me rather by surprise one morning when I entered one of these places and saw a youngish-looking British general, with his red hat on the back of his head and a book in one hand. I did not know whether to salute or withdraw. I suppose I dithered.

"God Almighty!" I exclaimed in amazement.

"Not at all," came the bland reply. "General Alexander; pray take a seat."

E.J. Gordon Henry,
Chairman, Stewart Wrightson Holdings Limited.

The rabbi was having great difficulty in finding some virtues to extol in respect of the deceased whose funeral service he was conducting. He asked the widow if she would like to pay a tribute to her late spouse, but she vigorously shook her head and remained silent.

The rabbi then asked the assembled mourners if there was amongst them one who would speak on behalf of the deceased. There was a lowering of heads and total silence.

"Surely," said the rabbi, "someone has something good to say about the dear departed."

Suddenly, at the back of the synagogue, one voice was heard:

"His brother was even worse!"

T. Cradock Henry,
Retired Consultant Surgeon.

An eminent surgeon practised at the London Clinic, which had, and still has, rather small consulting rooms. One day he received, amongst many patients, a youngish lady from Hampstead who was accompanied by her husband, her mother and father, all of whom crowded into this small room for the necessary consultation. In the end, Mr. D.W. pronounced the verdict that the lady was suffering from gall stones and would have to have her gall bladder removed.

After this sentence, they enquired his fee (one has to remember this was 1935), and he said it would be 150 guineas, whereupon they all went into a huddle in the corner of the room to have a conversation and came back with the answer that they would be delighted if Mr. D.W. would do the operation but could he possibly reduce his fee to 75 guineas. As he had another ten patients to see in the afternoon, he replied:

"All right, all right, I will do the operation for 75 guineas."

On the appointed day when he came into the London Clinic to perform the operation at 8 a.m., he found the husband waiting for him, who said:

"Mr. D.W., we have changed our minds, we would like to pay you your full fee of 150 guineas." Whereupon Mr. D.W. said:

"Too late, too late, I have only brought my 75 guinea instruments with me."

Sir John Herbecq, K.C.B.,
Second Permanent Secretary, Civil Service.

Mrs. McGregor was very worried about the behaviour of her teenage daughter, Jeannie. She took her troubles to the minister. Jeannie, she explained, had taken to staying out until sometimes two o'clock in the morning and now, to crown it all, she had acquired a very expensive-looking mink coat.

"What I want to know, minister," said Mrs. McGregor, "is, has she done right or has she done wrong?"

The minister was a wise old man and not given to hasty and uncharitable judgements.

"Whether she has done right or wrong," he said, "I do not know, but she hasn't done badly."

Paddy was in the habit of doing odd jobs for the priest, for which the usual reward was a generous dram. On one occasion the priest discovered to his dismay that he had run out of whiskey. He hunted round for an alternative and was able to drum up just enough Benedictine to fill a liqueur glass. Paddy savoured it, then remarked, half thoughtfully and half hopefully:

"That's a fine drink, Father."

"So it should be," the priest replied, "it was invented by the Benedictine monks."

Paddy digested that piece of information and then asked:

"And what Protestant b... made the glass?"

Professor George Hibberd,
Formerly Professor of Mining Engineering, Glasgow University and University of Strathclyde.

A teacher in a Glasgow suburban school was talking to her class about the metric system, explaining the various terms — centimetre, metre, kilometre, gramme, kilogramme, litre, etc. At the end of the lesson she decided to invite members of the class to compose sentences containing one of the metric terms. She then said to one little boy:

"Tommy, give me a sentence with the term centimetre in it."
Tommy pondered for a minute, then jumped up and said:
"Miss, my grandma came to see us last night and I was *sent to meet her.*"

Admiral of the Fleet The Lord Hill-Norton, G.C.B.,
Former First Sea Lord and Chief of the Defence Staff.

The virtuous man.
I am described by my friends as an exemplary man. I do not drink, seldom smoke, do not go around with other women, I go to bed early and I get up early. I work long hours and I take exercise regularly every day. I get no financial reward for this self denial.
All this is going to change when I get out of prison.

Dame Wendy Hiller, D.B.E.,
Actress.

I was lunching with Mr. and Mrs. Bernard Shaw at the time of the Abdication of Edward VIII and naturally the talk was all about it. G.B.S. was lamenting the lost opportunity of a union with the United States if the King had married Mrs. Simpson. Mrs. Shaw made disapproving noises. Then G.B.S. made what seemed to me a surprising statement.
"When the young fellow rang me up," he said, meaning the King, "I told him to do what Charlotte and I had done. Go to a Register Office in the Strand and get married. Nobody can stop you!"
I have wondered ever since if Mr. Shaw's advice was sound and if there is any other record of this amazing telephone call.

Sir Frederick Hoare, Bt.,
Lord Mayor of London, 1961–62.

Many years ago a Lady Mayoress of London, who was much concerned with correct social etiquette, was giving a dinner party for twenty distinguished people. Among those who had been asked was a well-known duke and also the Aga Khan.

After much searching the Lady Mayoress found that she was unable to solve the question of which of the two should take precedence at the dinner table. Accordingly she wrote to Debrett, who answered:

"The many millions of followers of His Highness the Aga Khan claim that he is directly descended from God — but an English duke takes precedence."

Sir Julian Hodge, K.S.G., K.St.J., LL.D., F.C.C.A., F.T.I.I., Chairman, Commercial Bank of Wales Limited.

A dear old Irish lady went to Confession, and as she was deaf she was inclined to shout. The priest told her to speak more quietly as all the people in the church could hear what she was saying. She yelled back at him:

"What did you say?"

So as best he could he told her that the next time she came to Confession she should write down what she had to say.

On the next occasion she knelt down and handed a piece of paper through the grille. The priest looked at it and said:

"What's this supposed to be? It looks like a list of groceries."

"Mother of God!" said the old lady, "I must have left my sins in Tesco's!"

The Hon. Sir Michael Hogan, C.M.G., Chief Justice of Hong Kong, 1955–70.

A diplomat is a man — or woman — who can tell you to "go to hell" in such a pleasant way that you actually look forward to the trip.

Introduced as a speaker with a warm commendation from the chair, my heart tends to sink when I remember the elderly relative, paying a long promised visit, who, on passing a bedroom door, was disconcerted to hear a small voice say:

"Mummy, why were we so looking forward to Aunt Millie coming to stay?"

Air Marshal Sir Paul Holder, K.B.E., C.B., D.S.O., D.F.C., F.R.Ae.S., Formerly A.O.C.-in-C., Coastal Command.

I was standing in the control tower listening to the R/T and chatting to one of my flying instructors. A number of our Iraqi pupils were going solo. Sending pilots solo is always a slightly anxious time. I could see that Flight Lieutenant Travers was not exactly at ease.

Travers had warned each pilot to keep the airfield in sight. A wise precaution, as visibility wasn't very good and the sky was overcast. I could see one of the pupils taxiing in, no doubt very pleased with himself and glad it was all over.

"Are they all back?" I asked.

"No. There is no sign of Pilot Officer Achmed. He can't have much more than ten minutes' fuel left. I think I'll give him a call. Hello, Red One. Hello, Red One. What is your endurance?"

Silence! Flight Lieutenant Travers tried again. Not a sausage. Time was running out. I looked round the horizon half expecting to see a column of black smoke rising in the air.

"Hello, Red One. Hello, Red One. What is your endurance?"

I could detect a note of anxiety in Travers' voice. An interminable pause. The R/T crackled:

"My endurance is the Prudential."

Three minutes later Achmed landed and ran out of fuel at the end of the runway. I was glad his executors hadn't got to claim against the Prudential.

**Lord Holderness,
Formerly Minister of Power.**

A club was holding a dinner in a hotel, to which a number of the guests had been invited to spend the night. It was thought this would make for a more convivial evening, without the risk of being breathalysed.

One of the guests, who had much enjoyed the evening, came down — rather late — to breakfast the next morning in one brown shoe, and one evening shoe. A friend remarked on this, to which came the reply:

"That is a funny thing, old boy, there is another pair of shoes just like it in my wardrobe."

Two gentlemen in their club.
First gentleman: "I was sorry to hear you buried your wife last week."
Second gentleman: "I had to, old boy. She died."

Professor William Holmes,
Professor of Agriculture, Wye College, University of London.

Observed in a Glasgow street in the days of horse transport, a somewhat drunken man watching a carter trying to adjust the nosebag on a rather fractious horse. Eventually the drunk can stand it no longer and blurts out:

"You'll never do it, you'll never do it."

"Never do what?" asks the carter.

"You'll never put that big horse in that wee bag."

Sir David Hope-Dunbar, Bt.,
Landowner and Farmer.

A speaker with socialist tendencies on a 'Brains Trust' panel when asked the definition of 'upper crust', replied without hesitation:

"A lot of crumbs held together with dough."

Admiral Sir Frank Hopkins, K.C.B., D.S.O., D.S.C.,
Commander-in-Chief Portsmouth, 1966–67.

The following story concerns an incident which occurred when I was commanding the Royal Naval College, Dartmouth, many years ago.

At a passing out parade a certain royal personage, having inspected the midshipmen, was presenting the Queen's Sword and the Queen's Telescope to the two young officers concerned. Her husband, who was standing in the background with a group of officers and lecturers and their wives asked what the telescope was awarded for. Nobody near him seemed to know and this evidently worried him.

After the ceremony was over I was introducing him to a group of midshipmen, the first of which was Nigerian, very black and some six foot six inches tall. Still thirsting for information he said:

"By the way, I saw my wife presenting a telescope to one of the midshipmen, could you tell me what the telescope is for?"

The Nigerian, obviously expecting a trick question, thought for a moment then drew himself up to his full height and said:

"To see distant objects more clearly, sir."

Brigadier John A. Hopwood, C.B.E., D.S.O. and Bar,
A.D.C. Bengal, 1935–37; Commanding 1st Bn. Black Watch, Sicily and N.W. Europe, 1944–45.

Distraught A.D.C.: "Sir, I have been with you for two years and can no longer stand the way your wife treats me. I wish to return to my regiment."

The Viceroy (placing his hand on the young man's shoulder):

"My dear fellow, I have stood it for twenty years, and I have no regiment to go back to."

Lord Horder,
Publisher; Author; Composer.

A very single-minded golfer was playing a friendly evening round when his opponent dropped dead of a heart attack on the third green. With some difficulty he lugged the body back to the clubhouse.

The next day some of his friends were commiserating with him at the bar about this dreadful experience.

"Yes, well," he replied blandly, "putting him down and picking him up at every stroke *was* rather a bore."

A mother and her ten-year-old son stood in front of Tintoretto's painting of the Nativity.

"What I can never understand," said the boy, "is why he wasn't born in a proper bed — after all his father was God, wasn't he, and ought to have been able to arrange something better than that manger, surely?"

His mother explained patiently that Mary and Joseph were on a journey at a busy holiday time, that there was no room at the inn, and that they were, anyway, very poor.

"Can't have been *very* poor," retorted the boy, "to get themselves painted by Tintoretto."

Michael Hordern, C.B.E.,
Actor: Stage, Films, Radio and Television.

Sir John Gielgud (to fellow actor): "I hear you are going to play Lear. Good, you'll enjoy it."

Fellow actor: "Can you give me a word or two of advice?"

Sir John: "Yes, get a small Cordelia."

Professor John H. Horlock, F.R.S.,
Vice-Chancellor, Open University.

On my first visit to the university, I lost my way in South Manchester. I stopped and asked an elderly policeman:

"How do I get to Salford University, please?"

"Young man," he replied, "you have to work very hard."

Alistair Allan Horne,
Author; Journalist; Farmer and Lecturer.

A very keen cricketer asked a divine, allegedly with good connections on high, whether there was any cricket in heaven. The priest replied:

"I can't tell you now, but if you come back on Sunday, I might have an answer."

On Sunday the priest told the cricketer:

"I've had good news. Yes, there is cricket in heaven. But now for the bad news — you are in to bat on Friday!"

Baroness Hornsby-Smith, D.B.E.,
Vice-Chairman, Arthritis and Rheumatism Council for Research, since 1974.

During a hectic cross country tour of remand homes when I was Under-Secretary at the Home Office, I was picked up at Exeter station by a police car and, as my third visit took me to Plymouth, where they had their own police force, I was met and accompanied by the Chief Constable. The remand home was a converted Victorian mansion with a semi-circular drive, and as we drew up some thirty young girls were avidly watching through the french windows. Seeing two gleaming black police cars, two police drivers, a chief constable and one female, one girl was heard to remark in awesome tones:

"Cor blimey, she must be a hot one. Two police cars and three cops to bring her in!"

Lieut.-General Sir Brian Horrocks, K.C.B., K.B.E., D.S.O., M.C.,
Former G.O.C.-in-C., Western Command, 1946, and B.A.O.R., 1948.

Cats look down at you, dogs look up to you, and pigs are equal.

**Sir John Horsfall, Bt., M.C., T.D., J.P.,
Industrialist.**

I recall during the war when I was at an Infantry Training Centre which was receiving new recruits for the Army, one new boy came to the Company Office after one week to receive his pay. In those days one had to sign on an acquittance roll which had numerous carbon copies, before receiving the pay. This recruit signed so lightly that his signature did not register through the various copies — so the Colour Sergeant in his Irish brogue said:

"Go on, man, put your weight on it," whereupon the soldier signed 'T. Jones — 10 stone'.

Pay parade ceased for a few minutes to recover.

**Professor William G. Hoskins, C.B.E.,
Retired Professor of History.**

The Rev. Baring-Gould wrote a hundred books besides *Onward Christian Soldiers*, for which he is chiefly known. He paid a curate to perform all the clerical duties, and in his ample leisure he sired fifteen children. He was rector of Lew Trenchard, in the wilds of West Devon. On one occasion he looked in at a village 'do' to give it his paternal blessing, circulated a bit, patted a little girl on the head and said kindly:

"And whose little girl are you?"

She replied: "Yours, daddy..." and burst into tears.

On another occasion, when I was walking round the whole of Devon making notes on the parish churches, I overtook on a steep hill an aged farmer slowly going upwards. I chatted with him and told him I'd just come from the church and asked did he remember Parson Baring-Gould. (He lived from 1834 to 1924, so most people round there would have known him.) Yes, he knew him well as both he (the farmer) and the parson were procreating at the same time. They made a joke (even a bet) that the parson would produce more children in the end but, said the old farmer:

"I beat 'un in the end. I had sixteen chillern, he had fifteen..."

Sir Edward Howard, Bt., G.B.E.,
Past Lord Mayor of London.

With all this 'to-do' over the Common Market, one of my fellow directors felt he ought to learn French and took one of those 'crash courses' for this purpose. He was naturally anxious to try out this newly acquired language, so at my Livery Dinner I sat him next to a French diplomat. For some time he was clearly at a loss to start the conversation — when a fly alighted on a glass and gave him the opportunity.

"Regardez le mouche," he said.

The French diplomat, who could speak perfect English, replied:

"*La* mouche, the fly is feminine."

My colleague was most impressed and turned to his companion on the other side and said:

"Goodness, don't these foreigners have remarkable eyesight."

Jack Howarth,
Stage and Television Actor.

A school teacher said to one of her scholars:

"Bessie, why did you not come to school yesterday?"

Bessie said: "Please, teacher, I couldn't come because my mum was having a baby."

Said teacher: "That's nice — have you got a baby sister or a brother?"

Bessie said: "A brother."

"How lovely for you. Do you know, I'd like a baby," said the teacher.

Bessie said: "Oh, it's very easy. All you have to do is — have a bath, put on a clean nightie, and then send for your grandma."

Two Lancashire lads won £500,000 on the pools and decided it would make no difference to their way of life. No more it did for some weeks, when one night over a drink, Bill said to Tom:

"Tom, dusta know what I'd like to do?"

Tom: "No, Bill, what would tha like to do?"

Bill: "I'd like to go to London."

Tom: "Reet. We'll go tomorrer."

So early next day off they went on a day excursion. Arriving in London they went to see Westminster Abbey and then to Buckingham Palace and also saw the Changing of the Guard. Then Bill said:

"Tom, dusta know what I'd like now?"

Tom: "No, Bill, what would tha like?"

Bill: "Some fish and chips."

Tom: "Reet. We'll have some fish and chips. Let's go and find a chip shop."

Having found a shop and having had a good feed they walked down Piccadilly and past the motor showrooms when Bill said:

"Tom, I think I'd like to buy a motor car."

Tom: "Reet, let's buy a motor car."

So into a showroom they went. The salesman came forward.

"Good afternoon, gentleman, what is your pleasure?"

Bill: "Flying pigeons, but we came in to buy a motor car."

Salesman: "Certainly, any special kind?"

Bill: "No. Just show us some."

Salesman: "We've got a nice Mini which has only done 750 miles. You can have that for £800."

Bill: "Nay, we want summat better than that."

Salesman: "Well, here's a Rover, only one owner. That'll cost you £1,800."

Bill: "That's more like it — but yon looks a nice one."

Salesman: "It is — that's a Daimler and that'll cost you £9,000."

Bill: "Reet. We'll have two."

Salesman: "Yes, sir. How do you propose to pay — by deferred payments?"

Bill: "No, I'll pay by cheque — £9,000 each, that's £18,000 in't it?" — and starts to write when Tom says:

"Hey, put that cheque book away. It's my turn. You paid for t' fish and chips!"

Lord Howick of Glendale,
Director, Baring Brothers & Co. Ltd.

As a young man, a friend's father, who was a district officer in the Indian Civil Service, started to get complaints from local farmers about marauding bears who were damaging their crops. Although reluctant to do so, he agreed to shoot a bear in the hope of discouraging the others. Plans were duly laid. Apparently, there was a ridge much used by the bears on their way to breakfast, and the idea was to get to a vantage point opposite before dawn to wait for a suitable opportunity to pot a bear as it ambled along the skyline.

What our hero had underestimated was the cold in the early hours of the Indian morning up in the hills, and in the event an hour's wait before anything happened reduced him to a shivering jelly. When the crucial moment came, and a handsome male bear appeared followed by an equally attractive female bear immediately behind him, he found himself clutching his rifle with freezing fingers and peering through a singularly unsteady pair of sights. He fired, and just nicked the male bear in the backside, who immediately stopped and sat down. The bear scratched his rump, then his head, and looked round at his spouse behind him. She was standing still, looking puzzled. Having, as he thought, worked out the cause of his distress, he turned round and gave her a tremendous cuff on the ear, before proceeding tranquilly on his way along the ridge. She, in turn, sat down looking distinctly aggrieved and rubbing her head.

After a few moments, she trotted sadly after her mate to take up her position docilely two feet behind him, shaking her head at life's unfairness.

By this time our hero was laughing so much that there was no question of him firing again, nor did he have the slightest wish to do so.

Sir James Howie, M.D., LL.D., F.R.C.P., F.R.C.Path., Hon.A.R.C.V.S., Hon.F.I.M.L.S.,
Retired Academic Microbiologist; Former President of the British Medical Association.

At a civic lunch I sat next to the treasurer of a city famed for its generous hospitality to visitors. As the waiters appeared with the second round of wine, the treasurer said:

"See now how the second round of wine divides the world into three groups of people. The first don't want any more, put their hands on top of their glasses, and shake their heads sadly: the poor fellas. The second look all round and about, pretending not to notice how their glasses are being refilled: the hypocrites. And the third group drain their glasses quickly so that no mistake will be made: chaps like you and me!"

**Sir David Huddie,
Engineer and Industrialist.**

Told to me by a Texan who later became U.S. Secretary of Commerce.

A native of Kentucky who was visiting Texas had been well wined and dined by a native of the latter state. In the course of conversation he said to his host:

"You know, we have enough gold in the State of Kentucky to build a wall one brick thick and three feet high clear around the whole State of Texas."

The Texan pondered on this piece of information and finally replied:

"You don't say. Go ahead and build your wall. If we like it, we'll buy it."

**Sir Havelock Hudson,
Chairman of Lloyd's, 1975–77.**

There are several ways of maintaining communications: I prefer the personal method, but there are many people who make use of mechanical systems.

It was my father's custom to take business friends to lunch, once or twice a week, in the restaurant of a large and expensive hotel in the West End. As a result, a friendly relationship of mutual benefit was established between my father and the head waiter, whose name was Mario.

My father died in the summer of 1952, but in December of that year an enormous envelope arrived on my box at Lloyd's, addressed to my father. It contained a Christmas card from Mario. I therefore wrote to Mario telling him the sad news. In December 1953 another large and expensive

Christmas card arrived, addressed to my father and signed by Mario. Assuming that he had not received my previous letter, I again wrote to Mario: I need hardly say I was in no position to go to such an expensive place for lunch myself.

When exactly the same thing happened in December 1954 I became rather concerned. I did not wish Mario to be left with the impression that my father was rude and unfriendly, so I thought it best to send Mario a Christmas card, signing my father's name. I felt better after doing this, and this process continued year after year until 1967. In 1967 I was invited by a rich business acquaintance to lunch at Mario's restaurant.

On arriving at the restaurant I told the waiter who brought the drinks that I would very much like to have a word with Mario. With an expression of considerable surprise and incredulity the waiter said:

"But sir, did you not know that Mario died in 1960?"

Professor John Pilkington Hudson, C.B.E., G.M., V.M.H.(R.H.S.), Former Director, Long Ashton Research Station, University of Bristol.

An African agricultural adviser saw a peasant farmer resting in the shade under a mango tree. He said:

"Why don't you stir yourself, work harder, plant more maize? Then you would have more to sell and you could hire someone to do the work!"

The farmer said: "Hmm, then what?"

"Well, you could sit back and take it easy."

"But, that's what I'm doing now!"

Two schoolboys were doing their homework downstairs. One said:

"We must be quiet because granny is upstairs reading her Bible."

The other asked: "Swotting for her finals?"

My wife and I were motoring on a road near a canal in Brecon and gave a lift to two boys who were camping on the bank. The canal looked rather deep, so we said:

"Can you swim?" and one of them said:

"We don't know because we haven't fallen in yet."

Lieut.-General Sir Peter Hudson, K.C.B., C.B.E., Deputy Commander-in-Chief, United Kingdom Land Forces, 1977–80.

A much loved officer who had commanded a battalion of his regiment with great gallantry and distinction for the last two years of World War II was the senior officer present when some students visited a particularly realistic demonstration by the R.A.M.C. Sights, smells and noises of the battlefield had been created in profusion and to the extent that one of the students fainted.

"What's the matter with him?" the colonel demanded.

"Oh, he'll be all right in a moment or two," came the answer, "he just doesn't like the sight of blood."

"Doesn't like the sight of blood?" echoed the colonel. "Well, what the devil *does* he like?"

Major Arthur John Hughes, M.C., T.D., D.L., Chairman, Hertfordshire County Council.

In Hertfordshire in the 1960s we opened a new sewage farm. After the opening and inspection we sat down to lunch, about two hundred at round tables of ten.

We were seated alternately lady and gentleman. I started talking to the lady on my left; we got on well. After a while I turned to the lady on my right but she was talking to the man on her right. I returned to the lady on my left. We went through the price of potatoes, iniquities of the tax system, etc. I turned to the lady on my right again, but she was still talking to the man on her right.

On the third attempt there she was, smiling, ready for a chat, and as I might appear to have neglected her I decided to give her my undivided attention and turned fully towards her, moving my right leg to the right.

At that moment, the waiter arrived with the coffee, and stood on my foot. I said:

"Waiter, you are standing on my foot," and the waiter replied:

"I won't be a moment, sir."

Field Marshal Sir Richard Hull, K.G., G.C.B., D.S.O.,
Lord Lieutenant of Devon.

Irate diner to the waiter: "What's this fly doing in my soup?"
Waiter (peering over diner's shoulder): "The breast stroke, I think, sir."

Christmas Humphreys, Q.C.,
Retired Judge of the Central Criminal Court.

A worried little man walked into a grocer's shop and asked for a pound of moth balls. The grocer sold him a pound of moth balls. A week later he returned and asked for another pound of moth balls. The grocer, somewhat surprised, sold him another pound. A week later the little man returned and asked for two pounds of moth balls. The grocer, now amazed, asked gently:

"You seem to have a lot of moths in your house."

"There are," said the now worried little man, "and you can't hit them every time."

Sir David Hunt, K.C.M.G., O.B.E.,
Retired Ambassador.

The chiefs of staff frequently suffered from this during the war.

We were working late in the Cabinet room. The P.M. could not keep off the subject of the atom bomb, as we called it then. Somebody had obviously been talking to him about it.

"From all I hear," he said, "the atom bomb, although it has a tremendous blast effect" — and he elongated the word 'blast' and spread his hands out sideways to give the impression of a wave of devastation spreading horizontally to great distances from the point of detonation — "has very little penetrative effect. In fact, if the atom bomb falls, what you should do is pick up your baby in your arms and take it down to the basement and you will be perfectly safe!"

He was still rambling on about the bomb when Christopher Soames came in. After greeting the P.M. he nodded to me and offered his congratulations.

"What's the congratulations for?" asked Churchill.

"David Hunt has just had his first baby," said Christopher Soames.

"Ah, then, he can take it down to the basement when the atom bomb falls," said Churchill.

Rear-Admiral Christopher Haynes Hutchinson, C.B., D.S.O., O.B.E., Director-General, Personal Services and Officer Appointments, Admiralty, 1959–61.

The daughter came home from school having had a lecture on sex.

Mother: "What did you learn today, darling?"

Daughter: "We had a lecture on sex, mummy. (Pause — mother somewhat worried.)

Daughter: "Mummy, do you and daddy have sexual relations?"

Worried mother: "Well ... yes, darling."

Daughter: "Then why have I never met them?"

Sir Peter Hutchison, Bt., Formerly Clerk of the Peace for East Suffolk.

After an uncomfortable night in a small inn a guest was eating an indifferent breakfast and tasting an egg which was by no means fresh, when the landlord came to his table and said:

"This is a very historic inn, sir. The great Lord Macaulay used to stay here."

Whereupon the guest quietly observed:

"I can only suppose that this egg was one of his Lays of Ancient Rome!"

Major-General Reginald Antony Hutton, C.I.E., D.S.O., O.B.E.,
Formerly Chief of the General Staff, Pakistan Army.

On the Nile in the garden of Gordon College stands an imposing statue
of General Gordon mounted on a camel. General Gordon is in full dress
with plumed helmet, medals, sword, boots and spurs. His camel, a
magnificent Sudanese beast, is gaily dressed in rugs with bells and tassels.

A small English girl who lived not far away used to love going to the
college garden and playing near the Gordon statue. In fact she became so
attached to it that she never seemed happier than when it was close at hand.

At last the time came when her father was transferred from Khartoum
and her mother took the little girl to the college garden for the last time to
say 'goodbye' to her beloved Gordon. There she stood enthralled, full of
respect and admiration. Her mother eventually led her away, and walking
slowly down the garden path the girl constantly whispered:

"Goodbye Gordon, goodbye Gordon, goodbye Gordon."

A short way down the road the little girl turned to her mother and said:

"Tell me, mummy — I've always wanted to know — who is the funny
little man on Gordon?"

Rutherford Graham Ikin, M.A.,
Headmaster of Trent College, 1936–68.

A man drove properly and circumspectly across the green light. As he
did so a woman, driving a stationwagon with 14 children in it, crashed
through the red light and the two cars collided. The man said:

"You stupid woman, don't you know when to stop?"

"Oh," she replied, "they're not all mine."

Brigadier Cecil E.R. Ince, C.B., C.B.E.,
Director of Warehousing, Ministry of Food and Agriculture, 1949–55.

When Sir Winston Churchill became First Lord of the Admiralty in
September 1939, he immediately became deeply involved with our anti-
submarine defences and travelled to Portland to watch a demonstration of
the famous 'Asdic' detector. He told this story afterwards:

"These fellows in the Navy put me on a destroyer and we steamed out in the Channel over an area where some wrecks were known to be on the sea bed. Sure enough, the 'Asdic' seemed to work. I asked:
'What happens now?' They replied that they depth-bombed the target.
'Well,' I said, 'go ahead and show me.'
"They dropped a large depth-charge over the stern and after a few seconds a great under-water explosion occurred and masses of water and wreckage were thrown up out of the sea. Believe it or not, up came a door apparently intact, but it had my initials (W.C.) on it. The Navy always knew how to pay proper compliments, bless them."

Sir Thomas Ingilby, Bt.,
International Lecturer, Historic Houses.

Texans have, even amongst the Americans, a reputation for being peculiarly eccentric and larger than life; there are more living legends in the Lone Star State than in virtually any other corner of the world.

I well remember Gloria; indeed, how could I forget, for at the age of 87, she still had the mind of a Nobel prize-winner, and for this alone I often wonder if she ever did exist — or was she merely a cardboard cut-out — a life-sized caricature!

In her youth she was a chorus girl in Paris — and managed to shock the unshockable city by growing the hair under her arms to such a length that she dyed it blonde and tied it in plaits, using ribbons to add to the decor.

She was happily married for many years — but not always to the same man. Indeed, her seven marriages were quite a remarkable achievement, Gloria having stolen all her husbands from their devoted wives; and, what is more, having buried all seven!

When I met her, she was happily planning her future. She had designed and supervised the building of a magnificent marble mausoleum in the local cemetery. It was air-conditioned inside and had one very well-considered item of equipment, unusual even amongst American tombs. It contained a telephone.

"But are communications with the dead really going to be that easy?" I foolishly ventured to ask.

"They may not get any easier by using a telephone," she replied, after a moment's thought, "but, my God, they're going to be so much cheaper in the evenings!"

Lieut.-Colonel Sir Berowald Innes, Bt., O.B.E., Seaforth Highlanders (Retired).

The war had recently ended: Irishmen and Jews were threatening the Prime Minister, and to blow up Government offices. Security precautions were in force in the War Office to which I had recently been appointed after commanding my Seaforth battalion in Germany.

I arrived one morning, checked through the security in the hall, took the lift to my office on the third floor — immediately over the Secretary of State's office — and opened the door. My table was bare except for a small battered leather dispatch case; something very unusual, as all papers had gone into my safe the night before.

I attempted to open the case but it seemed to be locked. I lifted it up. It contained something solid which rolled about inside. A bomb? I listened, there was no ticking.

No one in the next office knew what it was. I rang the War Office constabulary. In no time two breathless constables arrived; they too failed to open the case. Gingerly they rolled the bombs (they thought two) around. I suggested removal to a less sensitive spot. It was carried gently, almost reverently, to the lavatory down the corridor.

There we decided to force the lid. Bravely I got my fingers under the lid. Smooth, round, slightly greasy, certainly gelignite. The constable had a go — and agreed, certainly gelignite.

A nasty thought struck me. I slipped through the crowd that had assembled — but somewhat in retreat after the diagnosis. I got to my office and telephoned my subordinate upstairs. He had recently been my quartermaster.

"Norman," I queried, "back from Scottish Command?"

"Yes, sir," he replied. "Got in this morning."

"Have you left a case on my table?" I asked.

"Yes, sir, a present for you."

"Well, come down damned quick and open it!"

As I joined the crowd again, more confident, Norman appeared. He gave the lock a quick twist and opened the case.

It contained two haggis!

Fergus Munro Innes, C.I.E., C.B.E., Formerly Chairman, India General Navigation and Railway Co. Ltd.

The vicar was madly keen on golf. One fine Sunday he could resist the temptation no longer. He hurried through the service and slipped away to play a few holes on a remote part of the course where he thought he would be unobserved. Unfortunately St. Peter was looking down. Peter turned to the Almighty:

"Do you see that?" he asked.

"I do."

"Are you going to punish him?"

"I am."

At that moment the vicar teed up and hit the most tremendous shot he'd ever hit in his life, and holed out in one.

"What sort of punishment is that?" asked Peter.

"Ah, don't you see — he won't be able to tell anyone about it!"

Professor Peter Isaac,
Head of Department of Civil Engineering, University of Newcastle upon Tyne.

We engineers are notoriously bad at finding the right word, as the following story shows.

Two engineers from Newcastle upon Tyne, having a summer afternoon off, decided to spend it by the sea at Tynemouth. On the cliffs close to the ruined castle and abbey they found some donkeys and decided to take a ride. All except two of the donkeys looked rather bedraggled, and the engineers, after some argument, chose the two well-kept animals.

The donkey owners said that these two donkeys were normally kept for nuns from a local convent and had, therefore, been trained to answer to very special — and appropriate — words of command. They started at the words 'Good God' and stopped for 'Amen'.

Eventually getting them started the two engineers were enjoying their ride, and the donkeys managed a good pace towards the edge of the cliffs. Struggling for the right word, one of the engineers was able to stop his donkey, right on the cliff edge, with the command: "Amen."

On looking over the edge he could not avoid ejaculating:
"Good God!"

Professor Ian Jack,
Professor of English Literature, University of Cambridge.

In 1968–69 I found myself a visiting professor in a university in California famous for the high calibre of its 'faculty' and for its agreeable surroundings. At that time, however, it was no less famous for a severe outburst of student troubles. Half of the problems of modern life were being debated and contested, day after day, week after week. Policemen, sheriff's officers and National Guardsmen seemed to be everywhere — all heavily armed. To concentrate on one's work grew increasingly difficult.

One day I received a letter from the head of my Cambridge college — the only letter he wrote me in the course of the academic year.

"Dear Ian," it began. "A very serious situation has arisen in College." He went on to explain that it had been proposed that "ladies (underlined) should be allowed to dine at High Table (underlined) once a fortnight or even (twice underlined) once a week, in full term". This was so revolutionary a suggestion that he wished to have the opinions of all fellows, even those who were on leave. After reminding me that although the college had been founded by a bequest from a French countess, it did not follow that she would ever have tolerated such a proposal, the master concluded with a hint that I might well consider the matter grave enough to justify a flying visit to England to enable me to cast my vote.

As I was reading the letter a gun began firing outside. It was not the first time, and I knew what to do. I dived under my desk (a large one, as I was what is known as a 'Full Professor', as distinct from lesser species of the same genus), which was guaranteed to provide useful shelter. One of the two helicopters to which I had grown accustomed, swooped down, not far from the building (a building subsequently burnt down, probably by an arsonist). Having nothing better to do, as I lay on the floor, I began my reply.

"Dear Master," I commenced. "This is indeed a revolutionary suggestion." I paused, until the firing had died down. Then I continued by saying that so long as ladies made their appearance only once a week or preferably (underlined) once a fortnight, I thought that no irremediable harm would be done to the society. I mentioned that the return air fare from California was an expensive one, and wondered whether the college wished to help me to meet it from some special fund set aside for such emergencies.

I was then faced with the practical problem of posting the letter. Firing had begun again, and I did not wish to get caught in the cross-fire. It seemed best to remain where I was, if not necessarily under my desk. What to do? I remembered that the department of English, like all good university departments, was nominally run by a chairman but really run by a capable (and extremely personable) member of the opposite sex. I found my way along the corridor, avoiding windows, explained that my letter was an important one, and asked Alice if she could help me.

"Sure," she said, "you leave it with me; these things are just a matter of timing."

Sir Geoffrey Jackson, K.C.M.G., H.M. Ambassador to Uruguay, 1969–72.

The heir-apparent to an important industrial dynasty wouldn't settle down to his studies, and finally ran away from his university and vanished.

His distraught father hired the best detectives, who sought the boy for months. They finally located him working as a circus-hand at the other end of the country, in charge of elephants.

The father at once left by the firm's helicopter, and found the boy busy mucking out the elephant cage. After an affectionate greeting he implored the boy to abandon this youthful folly, and come back home and join the firm.

The young man stood there, leaning on his shovel, almost up to the tops of his wellies, jaw hanging, and exclaimed in horror:

"What, dad? And quit show business!"

White-haired old man, bumping into other white-haired old man rounding a corner:

"Good Lord — after all these years — it's Ginger!"

Lord Jacques,
Chairman of the Co-operative Union, 1964–70.

George (a salesman) went to London on business quite frequently and generally stayed overnight, returning the next day.

Out of the blue, his wife said:

"I believe you are going to London tomorrow. I would like to come with you."

He said:

"Oh! I shouldn't if I were you. I'll be fully engaged all day and you'll be on your own. Why not defer it and we will go up together without business obligations."

But she insisted and, of course, she went.

On the day, George bought a couple of theatre tickets before returning to the hotel, but his wife said:

"Oh, no, I don't want to go to the theatre. I want to go to The Alhambra Night Club."

George replied:

"You know I never frequent such places. Look at the publicity we would get if we got involved in any scandal." But she insisted, and so they went.

When they arrived the doorkeeper said:

"Hello, George, nice to see you again."

George told his wife that he had known the fellow when he had worked at a local hotel. Inside, the head waiter gave George a hearty welcome and conducted them to a reserved table near the floor. George told his wife that the waiter also had formerly worked locally.

A floor show was in progress and the ladies were by no means fully clad. When they came off the floor the leading lady made a bee-line for George and embraced him. At this his wife hit the ceiling. She said:

"Let's get out of here and go back to the hotel."

And, of course, they departed. In the taxi she gave him hell. On arrival at the hotel George paid the taxi driver, who said:

"I say, George, you've picked up a real bitch tonight!!!"

A well-known figure in the whisky trade died and there was to be a funeral service in a small Scottish town. The chairman of a large distilling company met the chairman of one of the smaller ones in a hotel immediately before the service. The chairman of the larger company invited the other to have a dram. He ordered two whiskies distilled by the smaller company. As they were hurrying off to the service the chairman of the smaller company, intrigued by the choice, enquired why he had ordered that brand. The other replied:

"Well, since we were going to a funeral, I didn't think we should smell of whisky."

Evan Maitland James,
Clerk, Merchant Taylors' Company, 1948–62; Steward, Christ Church, Oxford, 1963–78.

An American was visiting a remote village in Ireland in the hope of meeting a long-lost relation. Seeing a nice-looking pair of twin children playing in the street he asked them if they could direct him to Mrs. O'Donahue's house.

"That's easy," they said, "she's our mother and she lives over there."

So he knocked on the door and entered the parlour where another pair of twins were playing. He enquired whether Mrs. O'Donahue was at home.

"Yes," they said, "she is out in the yard," and sure enough, there she was, accompanied by yet another pair of twins.

The visitor, after explaining who he was, complimented her on her children.

"You sure have a mighty fine family, Mrs. O'Donahue. Do you have twins every time?"

"Oh Lord, no!" came her reply, "sometimes we don't have anything."

It is a fortunate thing for us men that wives usually outlive their husbands. No doubt that was why the other day a lady on a bus was overheard saying to her husband:

"George, if anything should happen to either of us you may take it that I'm definitely going to go and live in Bournemouth."

Walter James,
Principal, St. Catharine's, Windsor Great Park; Former Editor, *The Times* Educational Supplement.

Sir Robert Waley-Cohen, when he was Chairman of Shell, was asked why the company recruited so many young men who had got 'Firsts' in Greats (Philosophy and Ancient History) at Oxford.

"It is because," he replied, "they sell more oil."

Noël Coward was listening to a famous, even notorious, actress extolling her husband's virtues.

"As soon as I saw George," she said, "I knew he was the man I wanted to be the father of all my children."

"And was he?" Noël asked.

Sir Clifford Jarrett, K.B.E., C.B.,
Lately Chairman, Dover Harbour Board.

Here is a true instance of quick repartee.

A cross-Channel ferry was entering Dover harbour when the master spotted an advertising airship flying above him in the opposite direction.

Thinking to have a bit of fun with the port control station, he called it up on the radio and said:

"I have just seen an airship leaving the port. Did you give him clearance?"

Quick as a flash came the answer:

"No, sir, I'm afraid he went over my head."

As the dragon said when he saw St. George bearing down on him in full armour:

"Not more tinned food!"

**Clive Jenkins,
Trade Union Leader.**

"Small firms have smaller firms upon their backs to bite 'em
And smaller firms have smaller firms
And so on *ad infinitum*."

This piece of doggerel was written by Sir Harold Wilson and thrown across the table to me during one of the less spirited exchanges of the Wilson Committee to Review the Functioning of Financial Institutions, when it discussed the future of small businesses in the United Kingdom.

**Hugh Jenkins,
Writer, Lecturer, Broadcaster; Minister for the Arts, 1974–76; Director, Theatres Trust.**

This is a true story.

A few years ago a group of us were visiting the U.S.S.R. and were taken to what was called a Park of Culture and Rest. One of our number had been trying to score points off the guide and when we came to a great wheel he asked her:

"How is this thing categorised? Is it culture or rest?"

"I suppose," she replied, "that when you are going round on the wheel it is culture and when it stops it is rest."

The Rt. Hon. Roy Jenkins,
Joint Leader, Social Democrat Party.

I am reminded of a passage from an Oxford Union speech which Raymond Asquith, the short-lived son of the Prime Minister, made in the Oxford Union nearly seventy years ago, when he exhorted his audience to eschew any narrow, parochial or nationalistic approach.

"Let us rather," he said, "emulate the wide-ranging and refulgent generosity of that magnificent orb, the sun, which as all good Balliol men know, has for all humanity and from time immemorial risen over Wadham and set over Worcester."

Baldwin had a certain taste for anonymity, in one sense at any rate, and indeed achieved sufficient anonymity that at one stage fairly late in his second Premiership (a story I believe to be perfectly well authenticated) he was sitting in a railway compartment when the man opposite him leant forward and tapped him on the knee.

He said: "You're Baldwin, aren't you?"
Baldwin said: "Yes."
"Weren't you at Harrow in '82?"
"Yes."
The man said: "Tell me, what are you doing now?"

I subsequently heard, which I also believe to be well authenticated, the French version of the above, which I regard as even more extreme, when de Gaulle, as President, with his famous pear-shape, was making a ceremonial appearance, and suddenly saw somebody in the crowd. Leaving the Prefect, the Mayor — and everybody else — he rushed down, shook him by the hand and said:

"Dupont, Dupont, I have not seen you since 1914 when we were at the front at Arras together."

Dupont looked absolutely blank and de Gaulle said:

"Don't you remember, I was wounded alongside you and you carried me out, and Colonel Colombe was in command?" Dupont allowed slow comprehension to dawn over him.

"Oh," he reluctantly said, "then you must be de Gaulle."

126

The Late Rear-Admiral Sir Rowland Jerram, K.B.E., D.S.O., D.L., K.St.J., Deputy Lieutenant for Cornwall.

A very young boy aspirant for a probationary First Aid Certificate, when asked if he would explain the circulation of the blood, replied:
"Yes, sir — it goes down one leg and up the other!"

A similar girl aspirant, when asked:
"What would you do if your little brother swallowed the front door key?" replied:
"I'd climb in through the window."

"I've had a thorough check up in hospital. They examined my brain and found nothing." — Bob Hope.

"Laugh and the world laughs with you. Cry and you sell a million gramophone records." — Vic Oliver.

After a young married couple had just made up after their first quarrel, the wife remarked:
"I know I was in the wrong, darling, but I do think you might have apologised."

"If a man is not a Socialist at 20 he has no heart. If he is a Socialist at 30 he has no brains." — Maeterlinck.

**Sir Charles Jessel, Bt.,
Farmer and Landowner.**

It was during the time of our protracted attempts to gain admission to the E.E.C. Relations with General de Gaulle and some of his fellow countrymen were not at their best.
I was at Chartres with a group of fellow farmers and while viewing one of the beautiful doors of the cathedral got temporarily cut off. I found myself mixed up with some French tourists who were being shown the carvings depicting the Seven Deadly Sins and the Seven Minor Sins.

The guide described in French what each carved stone head represented. At length she came to 'La Perfidie'.

"And was this lady, who is so well depicted," she asked, "a real person who lived not too far away from Chartres at the time?"

"Of course," cried one of the French party in her own language, oblivious of my presence and to the delight of her compatriots. "It is obvious from her face that she is English."

David Dilwyn John, C.B.E., T.D., D.Sc., LL.D., Member of *Discovery* Investigations, 1925–35; Holder of the Polar Medal.

It was 1933 and we were homeward bound from the Antarctic, crossing a calm Bay of Biscay and finding ourselves to be in range on our radio set (the 'wireless' then) of the BBC. The third officer and I happened to be alone in the wardroom when the Corporation's Male Voice Choir (so I think it was) sang that wonderful old shanty 'Shenandoah', but sang it far too smoothly and perfectly for sailors' ears.

The third officer, who had spent a life at sea, beginning with years before the mast, and had been with Scott in the *Terra Nova*, looked sardonic throughout. When the singing finished he nodded fiercely to me and commented:

"Bloody fine sailors those; served two years before the microphone!"

Sir Ronald Johnson, C.B., J.P., Chairman, Fire Service Research and Training Trust.

There once was a lady who had been taught that, when you stay in a hotel, the first thing you do is make sure how to escape if there is a fire, so she put down her bag and opened the bedroom window. No escape that way; too far up. So try the corridor. Yes, a likely door at the end. But when she opened it, there was a man sitting in a bath.

"Oh, I am so sorry," she said, "I am looking for the fire escape."

"Try the other end of the corridor."

But before she reached it she heard the bathroom door open and there was the man, stark naked. So she ran for the stairs, circling down one flight

after another and the pad of bare feet behind her all the way. At the bottom she went straight across the hall and out of the front door. As she reached the outside steps a wet hand grasped her shoulder.

"Where did you say the fire was?" he asked.

Sir James Joint,
Retired Diplomat.
(Story contributed by his wife.)

The new Consul-General to the then Belgian Congo was a very short, nervous little man. He invited the Governor-General to dinner and on stepping forward to receive him, tripped over the carpet and fell flat on his face. The Governor-General looked down and with a smile said:

"Trop d'honneur, Monsieur. Trop d'honneur."

Hugh Jolly, M.A., M.D., F.R.C.P., D.C.H.,
Physician in Charge, Department of Paediatrics, Charing Cross Hospital, since 1965.

A four-year-old boy had been a great source of worry to his parents. He had spoken no words and yet was of normal intelligence and not deaf. He had been seen by many doctors, had many tests but all results were normal, so that the doctors were as baffled as the parents.

One day at mealtime he suddenly yelled:

"Food's bad!"

His parents were overjoyed and asked him why he had never spoken before.

"Food's never been bad before!"

Major-General Basil Douglas Jones, C.B., C.B.E.,
Formerly Inspector, Royal Army Ordnance Corps.

More than fifty years ago, when the railway was the normal means of travel, there was a Bishop of Exeter noted for his absent-mindedness. One day he was seated in a first-class compartment where his chaplain — having bought his ticket — had installed him, when the ticket inspector came along. The bishop hunted through his pockets but could not find his ticket. The inspector, who recognised him, said:

"That's all right, my lord, don't worry. I know you wouldn't travel without a ticket."

"Oh, but I must find my ticket," said the bishop. "I don't know where I'm going."

During World War II an enormous ordnance depot was established in the Egyptian desert. Acres and acres of stores — covering everything the soldier needed, from boot-laces to tanks, guns and wireless — were stocked. In that arid climate, where the moon came over the horizon like an enormous golden ball, there were many hazards of which the risk of fire was very great. To combat the fire risk, wooden towers, about fifteen feet high, were built and each one was permanently manned by a sentry with binoculars to watch a defined area. Each sentry had a plan of his area in front of him so that he could pin-point any occurrence and report it as being in A1 or B2, etc. He also had a direct telephone line to his nearest fire brigade.

One night a sentry picked up his telephone and shouted:

"Fire! Fire!"

The fire brigade naturally asked where the fire was and the excited sentry replied:

"Left of the moon."

Frank Judd,
Director, Voluntary Service Overseas; Formerly Minister of State, Foreign and Commonwealth Office.

Notice in a travel brochure about Switzerland:

'If you feel like participating in a sightseeing tour through Geneva you are welcome to it.'

Notice in the porch of a Hampshire church:

'As the maintenance of the churchyard is becoming increasingly costly, it would be appreciated if those who are able would clip the grass around their own graves.'

Professor Leslie James Kastner,
Former Professor of Mechanical Engineering, University of London.

An angry member of a golf club wrote to the secretary as follows:

"The Club Dinner was, frankly, lousy and I fully intend to bring it up at the Annual General Meeting."

Many years ago the officer commanding a British force sent to the North West Frontier of India received a despatch from H.Q. requiring a report on the quality of the water in the district. His reply was short and to the point:

"I have every reason to believe that the water is excellent, but I have noticed that it tastes strongly of whisky in the evening."

The writer, Michael Arlen, was complimented by a friend, an officer in the R.A.F., on the very splendid overcoat he was wearing.

"Ah, yes," said Arlen, "but you know how it is — per ardua ad Astrakhan!"

The Late Sir Bernard Keen, F.R.S.,
First Director of East Africa High Commission for Agriculture and Forestry Research.

There was a mandrill known as 'George', and his characteristic was a highly coloured posterior. The comment in a newspaper was:

"A chromatic colour scheme so disposed that everybody could admire it except George himself."

Air Marshal Sir Thomas Kennedy, K.C.B., A.F.C. and Bar,
Deputy Commander-in-Chief, H.Q. R.A.F. Strike Command.

A young man ran foul of the law in the Wild West and was hanged. A friend wrote and broke the news as gently as he could to the young man's family in the East:

"It is with deep regret that I have to inform you that your son died here recently while taking part in a public ceremony. The platform on which he was standing gave way."

Professor Edward John Kenney,
Kennedy Professor of Latin in the University of Cambridge.

Two professors booked into a convention. The first wrote his name in the usual way; the second merely put two crosses on the form.

"Why didn't your friend sign the form?" whispered the receptionist.

"Well, you see," said the first professor, "he's a sociologist, they don't have to be able to read and write. He always signs himself with a cross."

"But he's put two crosses; what's the other one for?"

"Oh, that's his Ph.D."

Professor Ivor Keys, C.B.E.,
Professor of Music, University of Birmingham, since 1968.

"On Christmas Eve we hymn the Birth,
On Boxing Day we mourn the Girth."

Lord Kincraig, Q.C.,
Senator of the College of Justice in Scotland, since 1972.

The female witness, whose appreciation of relevance did not impress the presiding judge, and whose longwinded answers irritated him to the point of intervening frequently during her examination, was becoming more angry as the questioning went on and on. Eventually she could stand it no longer. She fished into the depths of her handbag and produced a dead cat which she promptly threw at the judge. It missed. The judge turned to her and said:

"Madam, if you do that again, I shall commit you for contempt of court!"

Anthony King,
Professor of Government, University of Essex.

An American senator who received objectionable letters frequently used to reply like this:

"I attach a copy of a letter that I have just received. I thought you should know that some nut-case was writing to me using your name."

General Sir Frank King, G.C.B., M.B.E.,
A.D.C. General to the Queen, 1977–78.

When the first defence cuts were mooted, one famous regiment was engaged in taking some of its young soldiers to battlefields where the regiment had distinguished itself in the last war. The party had reached Anzio when the first savage details were published. Notwithstanding this, they roamed happily around the beaches, studied the various bounds of the bridgehead and then wandered slowly through the foothills leading towards Rome. Here they stumbled on a solitary tombstone, inscribed with no regimental crest but merely bearing the legend: 'Here lies an officer and a gentleman'.

One young soldier studied the inscription with special care and then, perhaps with defence cuts in mind, said with passion:

"My God! What are we coming to? Fancy burying two of the poor beggars in the same grave."

Air Vice-Marshal W.M. King, C.B., C.B.E.,
Senior Air Staff Officer, R.A.F. Maintenance Command, 1964–67.

At about 03.30 on a fine summer morning in the piping days of peace every air raid siren on the station came to life. As their dismal howls dragged on, officers and N.C.O.s gathered from all points of the compass intent on stopping the noise. Eventually the right switch was thrown, silence reigned and everyone made for bed.

However, the Station Duty Officer, who should have been among the first on the scene, had been conspicuous by his absence. Called upon to account for his lack of activity he explained:

"When I heard the sirens I thought: 'O God, a war's started and I'm Duty Officer! What am I supposed to do?' I turned to the Duty Officer's Order Book and looked for orders on the outbreak of war. Having searched carefully, and being only a little wiser than I was when I started, I realised that no bombs had exploded or guns had fired, so perhaps the war hadn't started after all. I telephoned the Guard Room and was told that it was surrounded by a posse comprising one Air Commodore, two Wing Commanders, five Squadron Leaders, numerous Flight-Lieutenants and most important of all for the protection of life and property — one fully-armed American Major. I decided that, with such a galaxy of talent already assembled, I could add nothing valuable, so I stayed where I was—in bed."

Scene: a mess meeting. Subject: should the piano be replaced?

A keen, serious musician argued that the piano was fit only for firewood and should go. An equally keen, but less serious, player maintained that it was adequate for all reasonable purposes. Snapped the serious musician:

"You know nothing about it. You only play by ear."

"Well," came the retort, "you only listen by ear."

Professor Albert Kiralfy,
Professor of Law, King's College, London.

In the last stages of the war in Europe I was one of a group of half a dozen N.C.O.s interrogating German prisoners of war at a P.O.W. camp. Soon after V.E. Day orders were received that on a certain weekend a few weeks ahead we were to pack up and proceed to London headquarters for other duties. This could have meant a movement to France or occupied Germany, possibly even to the Pacific where the war against Japan was by no means over.

During the winter several of the men had had leave in London and had acquired regular girl friends there. The group were to move in two jeeps to

London on the Saturday preceding the Monday on which we had to report, which left Saturday evening free. The minor inconveniences of the war in Europe being out of the way it now appeared that there was a major inconvenience still to overcome. It was pointed out that if the best uniforms were packed, as per orders, they would arrive in a crumpled state in London and not make a good effect at the dance halls. A suggestion was made that these uniforms should be hung on a rail and suspended in some way from a jeep. The senior N.C.O. refused to contemplate our arriving in the metropolis on a mobile clothing stall, but after heated argument a compromise was arrived at.

A hanging cupboard could be constructed by some skilled carpenters among the German P.O.W.s to accommodate the uniforms so as to keep them hanging tidily. It was visualised that this cupboard could be mounted on one of the jeeps so as to conceal its precise nature. The uniforms were carefully hung up and measures used to work out the desired dimensions. One of the group conveyed the details to the German Lagerführer, who, under some pressure, agreed to put the work in hand.

Several weeks went by without result, the Lagerführer protesting at the difficulty of getting the wood. Eventually, word came that the article was ready for collection. At this point our contact with the Lagerführer said that we should not worry about the job, as he had *doubled* all the measurements, as he thought they had been very skimpy.

One of the jeeps now drove, with some uneasiness, to the prisoners' compound. Our eyes were greeted by a huge structure which nearly blocked the gates! With the help of a number of prisoners it was manhandled onto the jeep after its superstructure had been stripped off. The jeep was then driven teeteringly for some distance to the edge of a small ravine and, with great difficulty, and well out of sight of the prisoners, tipped into it.

The reactions of the farmer when he went to re-occupy his land after the war are not known or recorded!

Sir Arthur Kirby, G.B.E., C.M.G., F.C.I.T.,
Chairman, National Ports Council, 1967–71.

A certain pop star had a great desire while he was in Rome to see and be blessed by the Pope. So he bought for himself a spanking new suit and joined the daily parade, but to his intense chagrin His Holiness passed him by without so much as a glance. However, a little farther down the line the Pope stopped and bent down to speak to a raggedly dressed tramp. Being an enterprising chap (as he had to be to succeed in his profession) the pop star made sure of meeting the tramp after the parade and offered him his new suit along with some money if he would let him have his rags. This the tramp readily agreed to, and the next day the pop star attended the parade dressed in the tramp's clothing in the hope that the Pope would notice him. He succeeded, for the Pope did indeed stop, bent down to speak to him and said:

"I thought I told you yesterday to buzz off and not come back."

Air Vice-Marshal Michael W.P. Knight, C.B., A.F.C.,
Air Officer Commanding No. 1 Group, R.A.F. Strike Command.

While flying across India some years ago, I was monitoring one of the local airfield control frequencies and had just heard an Australian call for a 'straight-in approach' on Runway 36. This was accepted by the Indian controller, who had asked him to call 'short finals'. A few minutes later, an Indian pilot called the same air traffic control tower and announced that he was 'downwind for Runway 18'. He was told by the controller to call 'finals', and was advised that the wind was light and variable.

After a suitable pause for reflection, the Australian voice was again heard:

"Lachmi tower, this is Tango Oscar: far be it from me to ruin your plans, you've just given that joker clearance but I'm on finals for Runway 36 and to land on 18."

A further, slightly longer, pause, followed by a very dejected Indian voice (the controller) broadcasting to the world his historic message:

"Oh, my God... another day — just like yesterday!"

Professor J. Alan C. Knox,
Emeritus Professor of Physiology, University of London.

In the course of experiments on the control of appetite, rats were trained to press a key which delivered a drop of liquid food.

In order to speed up the training process the experimenters hit upon the notion of putting a young untrained rat into the cage with an old experienced one which might possibly 'show it the ropes'. After some hours the recording instruments indicated that the key was being regularly pressed much more frequently than usual. Congratulating themselves, they went to the observation window to find the old rat reclining comfortably under the food spout while the young rat was pressing the key with the greatest enthusiasm.

Professor Sir Hans Kornberg, F.R.S.,
Chairman, Royal Commission on Environmental Pollution.

The minister of a particular department of state, being a busy man, had asked his private office to prepare a ten-minute speech for delivery after luncheon to a group of businessmen. Towards the end of his text, he noticed with dismay that he was not only losing his audience, but had spoken for nearly half an hour.

"What did you do, to land me in such a mess?" he asked his P.P.S. on returning to his office.

"I did what I always do, sir," his P.P.S. replied, "I gave you a top copy and two carbons."

Professor Eric Roberts Laithwaite,
Professor of Heavy Electrical Engineering, Imperial College, London.

Two American tramps were sitting beside a farm haystack eating their paltry meal and watching a cockerel chasing a hen round and round the stack. One of them tossed out a bit of breadcrust and on the next time around the hen went squawking by, but the cockerel stopped and ate the crust.

"Man," said one tramp to the other, "ah hope ah's never *that* hungry!"

Sir Lionel Lamb, K.C.M.G., O.B.E.,
Diplomat; Ambassador to Switzerland, 1953–58.

The club smoking room was almost deserted as usual at that hour of the morning. Of the three occupants, two were sitting together making conversation, while the other lonely figure was ensconced in an armchair at the opposite end of the room and hidden behind an open newspaper.

"I didn't know," one of the two declared during a lull in the conversation, "that the Archbishop of Canterbury was a member of our club."

"I don't think he is," replied the other. "What on earth put that idea into your head?"

"Only that he happens to be over there reading the newspapers," the first man insisted.

"All right. I'll bet you he isn't the Archbishop," challenged the disbeliever.

The bet having been accepted, it was agreed, after some argument, that the only way to settle the issue was to seek confirmation from the person concerned, and that who should do so be decided by the spin of a coin. The man who had initiated the debate lost the toss and accordingly approached the mystery man with a politely worded enquiry as to whether or not he was the Archbishop of Canterbury.

"Mind your own b....y business," was the testy reply. The enquirer returned pensively to his seat.

"We will have to call it a draw," he reported to his companion, "the blighter wouldn't tell me."

Sir John Lang, G.C.B.,
Secretary of the Admiralty, 1947–61; Principal Adviser on Sport to the Government, 1964–71.

As you will know, the crofters on the west coast of Scotland do a certain amount of fishing in between times. Some years ago a certain crofter found that he had caught in his net a young octopus. The creature flopped about awkwardly as the net was drawn in, causing the crofter to laugh. He decided that he would take the octopus home, where his wife and family found the creature equally amusing. They decided to keep him as a pet.

Inevitably they found that with his eight arms he could do a lot of things about the house, making himself useful in all kinds of household chores, so that the family reckoned that they were lucky.

One Sunday evening, the crofter, feeling at peace with the world and thinking that a little music would be nice, got down the bagpipes and commenced to play. After a while the octopus shuffled across and began to finger the bagpipes. The crofter, his curiosity roused, gave the bagpipes over to the octopus, who sat himself in a corner and proceeded to experiment with his new toy. After a while he seemed to get the hang of the instrument and was producing what would pass for pipe-music, at any rate to a Sassenach, when suddenly he groaned and then proceeded to shriek as though in pain. The crofter and his wife went over to see what was wrong and to their infinite surprise they found that, instead of the octopus playing the bagpipes, the bagpipes were now playing the octopus.

Peter was a pleasant enough child, intelligent and well behaved, but he *would* bite his finger-nails. His mother cajoled him, threatened him, punished him, but was quite unable to cure him. Then one day, on the verge of despair, she discovered that Peter had a morbid horror of becoming fat, whereupon she promptly informed him that the one infallible method of becoming fat was to bite one's finger-nails. The device worked like a charm, but it produced an interesting sequel a week or two later.

Peter was out shopping with his mother and, while she was examining materials in a West End store, he happened to notice another customer, a pregnant woman who was waiting to be served at a nearby counter. Fascinated, he stared at her until the stranger, embarrassed, eventually spoke.

"What is the matter, my little man?" she asked. "Do you know me?"

"No," replied Peter. "I don't know you, but I know what you've been doing."

Air Marshal Sir John Lapsley, K.B.E., C.B., D.F.C., A.F.C.,
Formerly A.O.C.-in-C. R.A.F. Coastal Command.

Doctor, pulling sheet up over patient's face and turning to anxious wife:
"First, the good news — his temperature has gone down."

The Irish garage mechanic, checking my trafficators, called out:
"It's working — no it's not — yes it is — no it's not — yes it is — no it's not..."

Professor John James Lawlor,
Professor of English Language and Literature, Keele University.

It is wartime London, and the blitz rages overhead as the British Academy chairman listens impassively to the guest speaker. The noise of descending bombs draws closer: and at last a large portion of the ceiling plaster descends.

Whereupon the chairman rises to lead the way to the air raid shelter with an apology to the speaker, whose discourse is nearing its appointed end:

"I regret, my dear sir, that our premises will not sustain your conclusion."

Sir Robert Lawrence, C.B.E., E.R.D.,
Chairman, National Freight Corporation; Vice-Chairman, British Railways Board.

As in most armies it was the custom in the 8th Army to publish in orders a code word to be used as a challenge to unidentified personnel approaching an armed guard. With this challenge a coded reply was also presented.

Whilst serving with the 8th Army in Sicily I was approaching a certain unit headquarters when a very Scottish voice said sternly:

"Halt, who goes there?" followed by two words which were quite unintelligible. Casting my mind back quickly, the last coded challenge I recollected was 'Desert Rats' and assuming these were the words used, I gave the prescribed reply which was 'Kill Italians'.

The small Scottish soldier lowered his rifle, which was pointing at my chest, and said:

"You've got it wrong, sir."

So I replied: "What is it then?"

He said: "I say 'Alex James' and you say 'Arsenal'," and added gratuitously: "You're the second officer who forgot it tonight."

Sir Christopher Lawrence-Jones, Bt., M.F.O.M., D.I.H., Central Medical Adviser, Imperial Chemical Industries Limited.

His colleagues were surprised to find the Professor of Statistics alone in the bar when they emerged from one of those conferences where a number of simultaneous events have been arranged.

"Ah, you see!" explained the professor blandly, "if I go to one lecture, I miss nine others. If I stay in the bar, I miss ten. The difference between missing nine or ten is not statistically significant!"

His Honour Paul Layton, A Retired Circuit Judge.

Many years ago I was appearing in a magistrates' court in the Midlands for a man charged with a serious and nasty offence against a very small boy. The boy, the magistrates had decided, was much too young to 'understand the nature of an oath' and would therefore give his evidence after a mere reminder that he must answer questions truthfully.

The prosecuting solicitor was being more than usually punctilious about asking leading questions, being unnecessarily careful not to appear to be telling the boy what to say. He got his name by asking what it was and that he lived with his mother at 10 Broad Street, but he could not get out of him the name of the village. Having tried several approaches and failed, he finally said:

"Look, Tommy, if I wrote you a letter I should put on the envelope your name and '10 Broad Street', and what else should I have to put?"

The answer came promptly: "A stamp."

Vice-Admiral Sir John Lea, K.B.E.,
Director-General, Naval Manpower and Training, 1977–79.

During my last months as a captain I was doing a tri-service computer course at Blandford — all students wore uniform and I was by far the oldest. We travelled by minibus each day between our accommodation and the instructional block. On one journey I noticed a young Pilot Officer staring at me across the bus. I asked him what was fascinating him and he asked me why I had a loop and a small metal becket sewn on my right shoulder. I explained that I had just become an A.D.C. to H.M. The Queen, and the fittings were for use with the aiguillettes.

"I'm so glad you told me," said the Pilot Officer, "I thought they must be to allow the parrot to get a better grip."

Two New Guinea tribes had been at war for generations and the original reasons were lost in the mists of time. A new and enlightened king came to the throne of one of the tribes and was determined to stop the war. He went to parley with the neighbouring tribe who, after a lot of persuasion, agreed that it was absurd to go on fighting when the reason had been forgotten for so long. A peace was agreed and, to celebrate, the enlightened king invited the king and the elders of his recent enemies to a banquet in his Long House.

When he got home his own elders were very apprehensive, and though they had to accept the banquet, they advised the king to hide the great golden Coronation Chair, a gift from The Great White Queen Across the Sea, and an object of universal envy by all their neighbours. The king agreed and the chair was hidden in the rafters of the Long House and covered with reeds.

The banquet day arrived and was a huge success. The rice wine flowed and the beat of the dancing became stronger and stronger, so that the whole Long House shook. The inevitable happened. The Golden Chair fell from the rafters onto the head of the visiting king, who not only acquired a splitting headache, but was also very angry at the lack of trust placed in him and his elders. The fighting started all over again.

The moral of the story is: 'People who live in grass houses should not stow thrones'.

Admiral Sir Henry Leach, G.C.B., A.D.C.,
Chief of Naval Staff and First Sea Lord.

A notoriously pompous and stuffy admiral was on his way by car to inspect a ceremonial parade, requiring his arrival to be precisely timed. After they had been going for some time his WRNS driver diffidently asked over her shoulder:

"I'm frightfully sorry, sir, but would you mind if I stopped for a moment?"

Furiously the admiral replied: "Nonsense, girl; certainly not; we can't afford to be late. Drive on."

She did. But ten minutes later, without further discussion, the driver pulled in to the side of the road in a thick wood, switched off the engine, jumped out and disappeared amongst the trees.

Several minutes later she returned, her face pink with embarrassment, got in, slammed the door, started the car, let in the clutch with a bang, and drove off.

The parade was made with seconds to spare. Leaping out, the driver flung open the rear door with a flourish and stood back, saluting.

And nobody got out.

While inspecting a N.A.T.O. warship at sea I asked a lone sailor on the upper deck what his job was.

"I am the Lifebuoy Sentry, sir," he replied.

"What," I enquired, "would you do if you saw one of your messmates floating past in the sea, having fallen over the side?"

Without hesitation he answered: "I should shout 'man overboard!'; I should seize the nearest lifebuoy and throw it over the side; and I should ring up the bridge and inform the Officer of the Watch."

Professionally entirely correct but almost too glib, so I probed him further.

"And what," I asked, "would you do in those circumstances if it was one of your officers?"

He paused for a moment, then looking me straight in the eye, said:

"Which one, sir?"

The Bishop of Leeds,
(The Rt. Rev. William Gordon Wheeler, M.A.),
Roman Catholic Bishop of Leeds.

In the middle of the 'thirties I was a member of the staff of a well-known public school. In those days it was the custom, which I think no longer obtains, for the boys to be punished for relatively small offences, by the writing of a number of lines, which had to be delivered on the Master's desk next morning.

In the course of a lesson I ordered one boy to do twenty lines for talking unnecessarily. The latter part of the lesson was a written exercise and I wandered round the classroom to see how they were all getting on. The boy to whom I had given the twenty lines had an unusually bulging pocket and on asking him what was the cause of this he produced a large packet of potato crisps. I had always had a great liking for these and told him if he would like to hand them over I would dispense with the twenty lines! This he gladly did. The boys were generally much better off than the Masters in those days and probably still are, for all I know.

Later on, for a much more serious breach of discipline, I gave another boy in the class 100 lines. Next morning as he entered the classroom I said:

"Boy, have you done that hundred lines I gave you yesterday?"

"No, sir," he replied, "but here are five packets of potato crisps."

Of course, I accepted them and it has been on my conscience ever since!

144

Rear-Admiral Ian J. Lees-Spalding, C.B.,
Formerly Administrator, London International Film School.

The students at the London International Film School made a film every term, and they could normally choose their subject. A Greek student came to say that he wanted to make his film about 'Pstofisee'. Not wishing to show my ignorance about the great Greek poets of the past, I fenced a bit and remained rather vague and non-committal. It was not until some time later that it transpired that what he actually wished to make his film about was the Post Office.

On another occasion a student came to me to say that he wanted Diploma (foreign students frequently omitted the definite article!). Although he was in his final term, I told him that he could not have his Diploma until the end of term when he passed all his examinations and so on. His state of agitation was clear as he repeated his request. At last he clarified the request by saying that the basement was flooding. What he needed was the Plumber!

Lord Leonard, O.B.E.,
Former Chairman of South Glamorgan County Council.

The Archbishop of Dublin was reading the *Evening Herald* and noticed in the 'Births' column that Mrs. Murphy had given birth to her twelfth child, so he sent for old Father Joseph and told him to take this £5 note and give it to Mrs. Murphy with his, the Archbishop's, compliments, as he always gave £5 to the woman who presented her twelfth child to the Church.

Father Joseph cycled across Dublin with the £5 note, knocked at the door and a woman appeared.

He said: "Are you Mrs. Murphy?"

She said: "Yes."

So he explained about the Archbishop's present of £5 to the woman who presented her twelfth child to the Church.

"Thank you," she said, "but I am a Protestant."

Father Joseph stared at her for a few seconds, and then said:

"Christ Almighty woman, have I cycled across Dublin to talk to a sex maniac?"

Air Vice-Marshal Harold G. Leonard-Williams, C.B., C.B.E., D.L., Chairman, Somerset County Council.

I was interested to read in last year's financial statement from a bank that they were 'on the brink'; and even more interested this year to learn from the accounts that they had 'taken a step forward'.

The Earl of Leven and Melville.

A Master of Hounds, when he died, left instructions in his Will that his body was to go to his hounds. The Hunt Committee was horrified at this last wish but hardly liked to disregard it altogether. One of them spoke to the huntsman about it and said:

"I really don't know what on earth we can do."

"Bless you, sir," said the huntsman, "that's easy. Have him cremated and I'll put his ashes in the hounds' porridge."

Sir Christopher Lever, Bt., Author; Naturalist.

The following question was once sent for adjudication to the Rules of Golf Committee of the Royal and Ancient Golf Club of St. Andrews:

"My opponent has hit his ball into thick rough; after searching about for it for several minutes I find it, pick it up and put it in my pocket. A few moments later I hear him say, from behind a bush: 'Ah, here it is.' What is my position?"

The late Lord Brabazon of Tara once wrote in the Suggestion Book of the Royal St. George's Golf Club at Sandwich, after a period of prolonged rain:
"That the water in the bunkers at the thirteenth be changed."

Viscount Leverhulme, T.D., Lord-Lieutenant of Cheshire.

A would-be film star went to her agent's office to obtain a job. When she got there the girl behind the desk asked her to fill in a form.

The first question on the form asked her name. This she duly filled in. The second question called for her address. This she supplied. The third question asked her to state her age. Here she hesitated, scratched her head, sucked her pencil and still did not answer the question. Then a voice piped up from behind the desk:

"I'd hurry up if I were you, every moment makes it worse."

Admiral of the Fleet Sir Terence Lewin, G.C.B., M.V.O., D.S.C., Chief of the Defence Staff.

There is a story told about Doctor Luns, the Secretary-General of N.A.T.O., when he was Dutch Foreign Minister. Before his first visit to Moscow, he received a stern briefing on the dangers of electronic eavesdropping and how he should inspect his room for hidden microphones. On reaching the hotel, he diligently set about the task; not a wire or microphone could he find. Bemused, he scanned the walls, the ceiling and the floor. Suddenly, he noticed a bulge under the carpet and, leaping to its edge, he lifted it to reveal a wire running towards the centre of the room. Seizing the cutters provided by his Intelligence Service, he snipped the wire clean through and, as he rose in triumph, there was the sound of an appalling crash from the room below as the chandelier fell from the ceiling.

Sir Anthony Lewis, C.B.E.,
Principal, Royal Academy of Music.

As a student at Cambridge I played the oboe and cor anglais in the University Musical Society Orchestra. One of my outstanding memories is of a visit of the great composer Vaughan Williams to conduct one of his works with the orchestra and C.U.M.S. Chorus.

This was a work in which there was some prominent cor anglais solos which at the rehearsal I thought I had executed not too badly. After the rehearsal the regular conductor, Dr. Rootham, kindly introduced me to the eminent composer with the words, "Dr. Vaughan Williams — this is the young man who has been playing the cor anglais in your work." Vaughan Williams, who was prone to be forgetful about aspects of his own music, looked at me in surprise and said:

"Cor anglais? I did not know there was one in the score."

He must have remembered later however, because he looked kindly at me during the performance.

Major-General Mike Lewis, C.B.E.,
Formerly Head of Intelligence at Supreme H.Q. Allied Powers, Europe.

Admiral Helfrich, then the gallant Dutch sailor, Commander-in-Chief in the Far East in 1942, was progressing rapidly up Main Street in Gibraltar en route to the Convent — the Governor's house — when an equally gallant but very drunk able seaman passed him without saluting. The admiral unwisely stopped the sailor and said:

"Do you not know who I am?"

Sailor: "You tell me."

Admiral: "I am the Commander-in-Chief."

Sailor: "That sounds like a fine job; you hold on to it."

Professor Uberto Limentani,
Professor of Italian, University of Cambridge; Wartime BBC Broadcaster
to Italy.

This notice, in peculiar English, was seen outside a hospital run by nuns on the outskirts of Rome:

"The nuns harbour all sorts of diseases and have no regard for religion."

The Earl of Lindsay,
Zone Commissioner, Northern Civil Defence Zone of Scotland, 1963–69.

Some years ago I was motoring in California. I stopped in a village to get a carton of cigarettes in the general store. I was served by a very nice boy just out of high school. It was in the days before hippies. Like all westerners he was very interested in any strangers, and said to me:

"Where do you come from?"

I said: "I'm a long way from home... I come from Scotland." He looked a bit startled, and said:

"How long have you been in this country?"

I said: "We got here about five weeks ago."

He said: "Gee! you sure picked up the language quick."

The Late Sir Martin Lindsay of Dowhill, Bt., C.B.E., D.S.O.,
Represener of Baronial House of Dowhill.

Before the Prince of Wales' first visit to the U.S.A. in 1921, he was preceded by an English con-man who sought to cash-in on New York hostesses to whose dinner parties he promised to bring His Royal Highness.

Part of his patter was that he was an Oxford rowing blue. One day, in the crowded bar of the Knickerbocker Club, he found himself talking to another Englishman, who asked:

"What number did you row in the 1919 boat? No. 3? 1919 and No. 3? Then all I can say is that you must have been sitting on my lap."

Sir Hugh Linstead, O.B.E.,
Member of Parliament for Putney, 1942–64.

Seeing from the table plan that I was to sit next to Mr. Churchill at lunch, I desperately tried to think up a subject with which to open the conversation on an elevated level. Our exchange went like this:

L.: "Those are splendid Kuan-Yins you have in the gallery, sir; what's their history?"

W.S.C. (a little suspiciously): "What do you call 'em?"

L. (pursuing): "Kuan-Yin — an Indian god, you know, whom the Chinese turned into a goddess. I've seen hundreds of these figures but none as lovely as these."

W.S.C. (encouragingly): "Say that name again."

L. (faint but tenaciously): "Kuan-Yin."

W.S.C.: "That's funny. Never heard it before. I call 'em Buddhas…"

Professor Henry Solomon Lipson, C.B.E., F.R.S.,
Emeritus Professor of Physics at University of Manchester Institute of Science and Technology.

A group of professors at a university decided that they must go on strike. They set up a strike committee to plan a course of action. But then one of them threw a spanner in the works.

"How will anyone know that we are on strike?"

A pair of progressive parents decided that, in order not to induce any inhibitions in their offspring, they would never refuse him any request that he might make. They were therefore rather taken aback when the child said:

"I want to eat a worm." So daddy went into the garden, dug out a worm and brought it in. The boy looked at it with distaste, but he did not want to change his mind so he compromised.

"I want it fried."

So daddy fried it. It still did not look appetising, and so the boy compromised again.

"Daddy eat half." So daddy cut it in two, closed his eyes and gulped down one part.

"You've eaten *my* half!"

In the days when women were only just being accepted in the older universities, some professors still objected; they would begin their lectures with the word 'Gentlemen' even if women were present.

One professor of geography was talking about a particular island in the Pacific which had an excess of men:

"Even women as ill-favoured as those present could have acquired husbands."

The women all rose in protest and started to walk out. The professor called after them:

"There is no need to hurry; the next boat does not sail for another week!"

Lady Geraldine Lister.

A commercial traveller arrived in town rather late one evening, in time for business the next day. He decided it would be a nice evening for a stroll, and as he walked along he looked up and saw the moon was up. A couple were passing at the time and the commercial traveller said to the fellow:

"Excuse me, could you tell me please if that is a new moon?"

To which the fellow replied:

"I'm sorry, sir, but I'm a stranger here myself!"

Sir Emile Littler,
Chairman, Palace Theatre, London.

Two men were having a chat about this and that and one said:

"By the way, I'm having terrible trouble with my lawn. I've got a mole in it, it's making a terrible mess and I just don't know what to do."

His friend replied:

"My goodness, you must get rid of it otherwise you are going to be a very unhappy man."

"Oh, I'll get rid of it all right."

A month went by and they met again.

"By the way, that mole, did you catch it?"

"Oh, yes," his friend replied.

"Do tell me what you did with it."

"Well, if you want to know, I buried it alive!"

Lord Lloyd, M.B.E., D.L..
Director, Lloyds Bank Limited.

A bishop visited one of the churches in his diocese and was somewhat put out to find that the total congregation numbered seven, including the choir. After the service was over he spoke to the vicar and complained about the small attendance, saying:

"That was a very small congregation this evening. Did you tell them that I was coming?"

"No," said the vicar, "but I fear the news must have leaked out."

Professor Seton H.F. Lloyd, C.B.E., F.B.A., F.S.A.,
Emeritus Professor of Western Asiatic Archaeology.

First lines of a schoolboy's essay on 'The Frog':
A curious bird the frog are.
When 'e leap 'e fly almost.
When 'e sit down 'e sit on what 'e ain't got 'ardly.

Air Vice-Marshal Basil G. Lock, C.B., C.B.E., A.F.C., C.B.I.M.,
Formerly Director-General of Security (R.A.F.).

As a young flying instructor at the Royal Air Force College, Cranwell, I heard many tales of the legendary Air Marshal 'Batchy' Atcherley — one of the famous Atcherley Brothers, who had earned the nickname of 'Batchy' by his dare-devil flying stunts. He later became Commandant of the College.

One particular true story was based on the fact that, in his off-duty time, Batchy was wont to frequent nearby pubs wearing a highly disreputable sports jacket and flannels and blending readily with the local scene. One night he was engaged in conversation with a young R.A.F. corporal stationed at Cranwell and he elicited a great deal of information about his establishment from 'the other side of the fence' as it were. Posing as a worker on an estate he even gave the corporal a lift back to the R.A.F.

College after closing time, and as they parted in good spirits and the best of friends, the corporal's final words were:

"Thanks a lot. Goodnight, cock."

The following morning happened to be the day of the Commandant's Parade, and as Batchy's car came to a halt, out he stepped in dress uniform, complete with sword, full regalia and, of course, a formidable row of medals. He acknowledged the salute of the Parade Commander and then, stepping straight through the first rank, found his companion of the night before. Clapping one hand on his shoulder he said:

"Morning, cock," and carried on with the inspection!

A German U-boat surfaced off the coast of Italy in World War II, and the captain, hailing a nearby Italian vessel, asked:

"Is the war over yet?"

On receiving a negative answer he just had time to call before crash diving:

"Mein Gott — the Kaiser — what a hard man is he!"

A United States Navy fighter pilot belonging to an aircraft carrier group in the Pacific in World War II had a number of misdeeds, crashes and near crashes to his credit. His captain sent for him and after delivering a severe reprimand stated that, unless his performance improved dramatically, he would be thrown out. That very afternoon the pilot had been out on patrol for some twenty minutes when down below he saw five aircraft attacking one of the carriers. He carefully stalked the leader and shot him down from behind. He dealt similarly with number two and number three, both of which went down in flames. Numbers four and five left in a hurry! After a couple of victory rolls over the top of the carrier the pilot landed aboard, stopped engine, dashed up to the bridge, saluted the captain and said:

"Some performance, eh, Captain? What do you think of that?"

"Ah," replied the captain, "velly intelesting, you Amelican svine."

Miss Margaret Lockwood,
Actress.

The luncheon was given by Sir J. Arthur Rank in a large marquee in the grounds of Pinewood. A.E. Matthews was sitting at my table, and after lunch there were several short and witty speeches — one by Wilfrid Hyde White who is brilliant at this sort of thing. Unfortunately the last speaker was an accountant of the company who went on and on and on. Everyone was getting bored and restless, and finally 'Matty' said in a very loud voice:

"Good God, doesn't the fellow realise I haven't long to live?"

Lieut.-Colonel John Logan, T.D.,
Vice-Lieutenant, Stirlingshire, 1965–79.

My son and I went on the Siberian railway to China in 1977 and towards the end of our three weeks' stay there found ourselves having dinner in the restaurant of a hotel in that most beautiful city of Hangchow, in Central China. It was national spring cleaning week in all China's hotels and most of the restaurant's furnishings were stacked away in a corner, leaving us, with one or two others, sitting in the middle of a large empty space.

Soon after we had started dinner, a party of ten foreigners came in, closely shepherded by four Chinese; they disappeared through a side door.

"Those people looked to me as if they might have been British," I said to my son.

"Yes, I think so too," he said, and we thought no more about it.

The next day we boarded a train for Shanghai and found in our coach a party which closely resembled the one we had seen the previous evening in the restaurant.

"I think they look like school teachers," I whispered to my son. "That rather fierce looking woman must be the headmistress of a girls' school, the man next to her, in all probability, is a teacher in a secondary school, and the tall man doing all the talking undoubtedly a master in a public school." The train rumbled on and again we thought no more about it until, lo and behold, there they were again on the Air France aeroplane going back to Europe, comfortably ensconced in the V.I.P. section.

During a stop of two hours at Peking passengers were allowed out into the spacious, palatial waiting hall. My son and I were sitting together watching the people, when he suddenly said to me:

"That man standing over there, dad, with his hands clasped behind his back, doing all the talking with the man with him, is the one we thought was the master from a public school. I'll bet you that at any moment he will go up and down on his toes several times — all schoolmasters do it; it seems to give them a feeling of self importance." Within seconds the man was doing just that very thing; we had proof positive at last. Our judgement had been vindicated.

Back on the aeroplane an insatiable curiosity began to gnaw at my vitals. I could no longer resist the temptation to get final confirmation that our theory was right so I edged my way along to the V.I.P. compartment, to find one seat empty next to a man reading a book. I sat down and said:

"Please forgive my intrusion. My son and I have been following the movements of your party for the past three days, and thought you must have something to do with education and wanted to see if our judgement was right."

"Perfectly right," he replied, "I am the Vice-Chancellor of Durham University; we have with us the Vice-Chancellor of Oxford, the Regius Professor of Physics at Cambridge and the Chairman of the British Council."

We may have been vindicated but perhaps not in the way we had expected.

Air Vice-Marshal Francis William Long, C.B., D.L.,
Formerly A.O.C. 23 Group, 1952–53.

When Admiral Cunningham was C.-in-C. Mediterranean during the war he was made a K.C.B. He was already a K.B.E.

On seeing the announcement, his friend, Admiral Somerville, sent him the following signal:

"Heartiest congratulations. Fancy — twice a Knight at your age!"

Sir Gilbert Longden, M.B.E.,
Member of Parliament for S.W. Hertfordshire, 1950–74.

An M.P. explaining the 'brain drain':
"It's quite simple. The Chancellor applies the screw, and as they're not nuts, they bolt."

At a performance of 'Faust' at the Abbey Theatre, Dublin, the trap-door stuck, permitting only the lower half of Mephistopheles to disappear into the nether regions.
A voice from the gallery:
"Hurrah, boys, hell's full!"

The Hon. Ivor Lucas, C.M.G.,
H.M. Ambassador to Oman.

In the summer of 1972, Prime Minister Edward Heath visited Copenhagen with the object of persuading the Danes to join the European Economic Community with us. It was a highly successful visit, with Mr. Heath in sparkling form throughout. On the last evening the Social Democrat Danish Prime Minister gave a lavish banquet for his Conservative opposite number in the magnificent setting of Christiansborg Castle.

Towards the end of the meal, Mr. Krag rose to propose a toast to his guest. It was a brilliant and witty speech in the best British after-dinner style — and in perfect English — based on the experiences of King Christian of Denmark when he visited King James of England in 1604: the retinue he brought, the revelries they enjoyed, and so on. I sat listening with admiration — but also with trepidation, since I knew what a turgid script we had prepared for Mr. Heath, and could not see how he was going to match this. But I need not have worried. When Mr. Krag eventually sat down, Mr. Heath got up, and began:

"Mr. Prime Minister. We have all listened with amusement and instruction to your fascinating excursion into history. I only wish, Mr. Krag, that I had the staff to do the same for me!"

After this sally, and more in similar vein, he had the audience eating out of his hand, and the serious part of his speech went down as easily and as well as the dessert.

Major-General Robert Beverley Loudoun, C.B., O.B.E., Royal Marines (Retired); Director, Mental Health Foundation.

Three old Frenchmen were sitting in the spring sunshine bemoaning the effects of old age. The first, a mere 60-year-old, complained:

"As a lover of music I find I cannot now appreciate the full range of sound; my hearing has lost its acuteness; ah, my friends, deafness is a terrible thing."

The second, some ten years older, returned:

"All my life I have had great joy from an appreciation of painting but now, on my visits to the Louvre, my eyes cannot see the delicate shades and tones; loss of sight is a far more frightening failing."

"Ah, my poor young friends," said Jacques, a nonagenarian, "you have not begun to understand the true meaning of old age. Yesterday I awoke alongside my mistress, Fifi; the sunlight was playing on her bosom and I was filled with desire. I woke her. 'Fifi,' I said, 'I wish to make love...'

'You old fool,' she replied, 'only five minutes ago...'

"Oh, my friends, the memory, it fails."

Sir Henry Lushington, Bt.,
Formerly Superintendent, Metropolitan Police; Flt.-Lieutenant R.A.F.V.R.

Sunday supper is always an informal meal with my family; one weekend we had asked a young man down. On the Sunday evening at about eight o'clock my elder daughter said:

"I hope you don't mind, Nicholas, but we always have Sunday supper on our knees."

She, her younger sister and my wife left the room to fetch the food, and I was busy getting the drinks. On their return to the room they found Nicholas kneeling down in front of his chair waiting for his supper!

Sir Robert Lusty,
Publisher.

A famous author of many best-sellers died and in his Will requested that ten per cent of his ashes should be scattered over his literary agent.

Sir Rudolph Lyons, Q.C.,
Circuit Judge and Honorary Recorder of Manchester.

Some of you may recall the elevation to the High Court Bench of a judge of Scottish origin who was renowned, in addition to his professional capabilities, for his addiction to his native tipple. In announcing his appointment, a national newspaper, omitting the letter 'c', referred to him as 'the well-known Sot'. His wife asked him what he was going to do about it. He was silent for some time and then delivered what was to prove his shortest judgement:

"Nothing," he replied, "I shall just sit tight."

Sir Patrick McCall, M.B.E., T.D.,
Clerk of the Lancashire County Council, 1960–72.

I spent most of my working life in Lancashire with the County Council of which I was for some time Clerk. I was also Clerk of the Peace, the 26th and last, and also Clerk of the Lieutenancy. In that capacity I was concerned

158

with many royal visits. The King or Queen when in Lancashire frequently visit the Duchy Estates in their capacity of Duke of Lancaster.

King George VI on, I think, his last visit, was at a Duchy farm and being shown round by the farmer. The King saw a cow he particularly admired and said to the farmer:

"That cow has a fine face."

The farmer replied: "Aye, King, but t'other end's business end."

Professor Donald Neil MacCormick,
Regius Professor of Public Law, Edinburgh University.

The late Oliver Brown used to regard it as a matter both of geometry and of history that when the Angles first landed in Northumberland, the acute Angles turned north and became Scots while the obtuse Angles turned south and became English.

It is sometimes doubted whether there remains any form of witchcraft in Scotland. The doubt was resolved for me by a friend who gave the following report.

He was travelling towards Oban from Glasgow on a very dark rainy night in the autumn. As he passed up the road near Tyndrum he saw a beautiful young woman trying to thumb a lift. She was soaked to the skin and shivering and her long blonde hair was quite strikingly attractive.

But it turned out that she was a witch. The evidence was as follows:

They were travelling along the road for half a mile or so having a certain amount of conversation, when she touched the driver on the knee and he turned into a lay-by.

Professor MacNeile Dixon, of Glasgow University, was a great lecturer and wit, though always somewhat dilatory about marking and commenting on his students' written work. One day, he happened to open his lecture with the words:

"Gentlemen, Hazlett once wrote an essay…" As he paused for effect, a voice from the back row called out:

"Did he ever get it back from the professor?"

The Hon. Lord MacDonald, M.C.,
Senator of the College of Justice in Scotland.

An old Scots minister, on a motoring holiday up north, found himself caught in a thick Highland mist as dusk fell, and was soon lost. As luck would have it, a few yards further on he spied the light from a cottage window, and there he sought directions.

The cottager, a shepherd, and his wife insisted that he stay the night for safety, and offered him board and bed, the latter to be shared with their small son.

After a splendid meal provided by his hostess he gratefully retired to bed with his small companion. He undressed quickly and got into bed when, suddenly, in the candle-light, he noticed the boy kneeling at the bedside and, as the realisation that the child was saying his prayers — an office he had himself omitted — dawned on him, he shamefacedly crept from under the covers to kneel on the other side.

"My maw'll gie ye hell the morn," said the wee lad. "The po's this side."

Two private soldiers, serving with the Argyll and Sutherland Highlanders in the last war, were separated from their platoon during a desert action.

They struggled through the sand, under a blazing sun until, exhausted, they sat down in the shade of a sand dune to draw breath and take stock of their position.

"D'ye ken whit day this is?" reflected Sandy.

"Naw," answered Jock, "whit?"

"It's the Cowal Games, the day," said Sandy, "that's whit."

"Och, so it is," mused Jock. "Man, they're havin' a rare day for it."

Professor Gavin MacDonald, F.R.S.E.,
Professor of Physics, University of Dundee.

To determine the qualification one requires to do a particular job is a task fraught with difficulty, as the following story shows.

Beauly is a small town just north of Inverness and which has two claims to distinction. One is that I was born there; the other that it is the home of the Lovat Scouts, who played a significant part in the last war, particularly in the formation of the Commandos.

Kenneth, a good friend of mine, was in Beauly some time ago having a drink in a pub with a local Beauly man. They were joined by a second local who was introduced as the secretary of the Lovat Scouts' Association. He was soon bemoaning the fact that he was having the usual difficulty in arranging the annual Lovat Scouts' Reunion Dinner, since nobody wanted to travel that far north at that time of the year.

"Ach, now," said the first Beauly man, "my friend Kenneth is a very fine after-dinner speaker and I am sure he would be delighted to come up and help you out if you're really stuck."

The Lovat Scout brightened visibly.

"Would you be good enough to give us a wee bit crack on that evening?" he asked.

Kenneth, feeling that he was being got at, saw no way out.

"If you're really stuck," he said reluctantly, "I suppose I could give you a helping hand. But you realise it would cost you quite a bit."

"Do you mean you charge for that sort of thing?" asked the Highlander cautiously.

"I don't actually charge," Kenneth explained, "but I'd expect to be treated right royally during the course of the evening."

"Now what would you mean by right royally?" asked the Lovat Scout.

"Well, during the course of the evening I'd expect to be plied with, say, a dozen malt whiskies."

"Ach," said the Lovat Scout in disgust. "At that rate you're not even qualified to be present."

Sir Peter Macdonald, D.L., W.S., Industrialist.

A business man had occasion to spend a day in the country to keep an appointment and travelled by train. He had a few hours to pass in the middle of the day before he caught his return train, so he said to the stationmaster:

"How does one put in a couple of hours here?"

The stationmaster replied:

"We have got a cricket pitch."

"Where is it?" asked the visitor.

"Behind the station," came the reply.

So they proceeded to the pitch and the visitor went in to bowl, the stationmaster to bat, and the porter to field. In no time at all the stationmaster was bowled out, at which the porter threw his hat in the air and danced about in great glee. This puzzled the visitor, who said:

"What's all the excitement?"

"The excitement," the porter said, "is that the b——'s been *in* for three years!"

Dr. Gordon Peter McGregor,
Principal of the College of Ripon and York St. John.

The middle-aged father couldn't really fathom the depth of his adolescent daughter's passion for horses. Eventually he exploded:

"Now look here, Belinda, this has gone far enough. The house is littered with tack and pony magazines. You're late for every meal. You never wear anything but jacket and jodhpurs. You talk of nothing but horses. Your hair looks like a horse's mane — and now I get near you, girl, I'm damned if you're not beginning to *smell* like a horse!"

At this last thrust Belinda smiled ecstatically and said:

"Oh, daddy — *thank you!*"

Teachers expect to have the last word but just occasionally creative indiscipline triumphs.

Johnnie, being a natural actor, had been given the key role of Joseph in the Nativity play. But he fooled about and ad-libbed so outrageously that the class teacher determined to sort him out.

"Right, young man. You may think you're Danny Kaye but you're *not* going to be Joseph. You can be the inn-keeper. That gives you exactly two words and I hope you make the most of them!"

Johnnie sulked through rehearsals, but bided his time.

Came the great day of the performance. The school hall was packed with fond parents, offspring and, of course, the headmistress, confidently awaiting the usual success and congratulations.

All went swimmingly until Mary and Joseph arrived in Bethlehem.

Joseph rapped on the inn door. Johnnie appeared.

"Have you any room?" said Joseph.

Johnnie grinned. "Yes," he said. "Plenty!"

Professor Donald M. MacKay,
Research Professor of Communication and Neuroscience, University of Keele.

Ethnic jokes are out of fashion, so here is a non-ethnic one.

A non-ethnic person (let's call him Paddy), peaceably enjoying his pint, was offered a riddle by a barman.

"My mother had a child. It wasn't my brother; it wasn't my sister. Who was it?"

Paddy scratched his head without success.

"It was me, ye fool!" said the barman.

Paddy thought that was a good one, and tried it on his wife Mary when he got home.

"My mother had a child. It wasn't my brother; it wasn't my sister. Who was it?"

Mary was flummoxed. Paddy was triumphant:

"It was George at the Rose and Crown, ye fool!"

Sandy and Jock were on holiday, and hired a boat to go fishing on the lake. They found a marvellous stretch of water, teeming with fish.

"We'il hae to come back here tomorrow," said Sandy. "Mark the spot so we'll know it again."

"Right-oh," said Jock.

At the landing stage Sandy thought he'd better double check.

"Are you sure you marked that spot, Jock?"

"Aye — I made a nick wi' ma knife right here on the side o' the boat."

"Och, you gomeril! What if we dinna get the same boat tomorrow?"

**Air Commodore Alastair Mackie, C.B.E., D.F.C. and Bar,
Director-General of the Health Education Council.**

The after-dinner speaker droned on and on and on.

A bored and tipsy diner became so embarrassingly disruptive that his neighbour, feeling he had to do something, asked a waiter to bring him some black coffee.

"Yes, please do," said the offender in a voice that echoed round the room. "And while you're at it, bring some toast and marmalade as well."

**Brigadier Gilbert R. McMeekan, C.B., D.S.O., O.B.E., J.P.,
Chief Superintendent, M.E.X.E. Christchurch, 1946–50.**

The pilot was making the usual,
"Coming in to land at Sydney shortly"
speech after a very long, hot flight with
many delays. Without switching off
the intercom he added to his co-pilot: "And
what I want is a cold beer and a hot sheila."

A stewardess, rushing up to tell him
to switch off, was greeted with a cry:

"Hey, you've forgotten the beer."

A French visitor was asked whether he would like to accompany his host to a Golden Wedding. This phrase was unfamiliar and had to be explained to him.

"Fantastique!" he exclaimed. "Fifty year they live together and now they marry."

The burly surgeon was hammering away up my nose under a local anaesthetic. After a juddering, but hitherto painless, eternity he said to his assistant:

"Give me that large chisel, the one I don't often use."

Lord Mackie of Benshie, C.B.E., D.S.O., D.F.C.,
Former Member of Parliament for Caithness; Chairman, Caithness Glass Ltd.

A young boy was engaged in the time-honoured job of pulling turnips with the foreman of a farm in Aberdeenshire. It was a cold day and he complained to his boss about the extreme cold of the turnip shaws. The only reply he received was:

"Ah, weel, dinna haud them sae lang."

When I was fighting the 1964 General Election in Caithness, two of my lady supporters went canvassing in the deep country. They came to an old thatched house and an old lady of eighty-odd summers, smoking a clay pipe, came to the door. One lady launched into a description of Liberal philosophy, leading to Liberal policy, the Common Market, etc. After several minutes she saw she was having no effect, so she stopped and said:

"Anyhow, you should vote for George Mackie. He is the best man."

Whereupon the old lady's eyes gleamed and, seizing the canvasser by the arm, said:

"Hoo dae ye ken — have ye tried him?"

George Mackley,
Headmaster, Sutton East Secondary School and Art Department, 1953–60.

An old friend, a retired opera and oratorio singer, amused himself by hunting for old paintings and drawings at the Caledonian Market. In his innocence, he thought that if he dressed in old clothes and called everybody 'Guv'nor', the cockneys would take him for one of themselves and allow him to buy antiques at a cheap rate. But his rich and sonorous voice and accent betrayed him and provided the salesmen with much secret amusement. One of these offered to sell him a lawn mower, but my friend declined it saying:

"It's of no use to me. I have no garden."

The answer came: "Never mind, Guv'nor, take it out on the common for a day."

I told a friend the above story, but he could beat it with a better one about cockney humour, which he told me:

He moved from the North Country to take an appointment in the outer London area. He travelled on a country bus to his place of business and entered into conversation with the conductor, to whom he said:

"I thought that London buses were red, but this one is *green*."

To this the conductor replied:

"Don't worry too much about that, Guv'nor — a few more days of this fine weather and she'll soon ripen off."

Lord MacLeod of Fuinary, M.C.,
Founder of the Iona Community, Scotland.

In the first half of the last century, Scotland was very religious. Four hundred ministers of the Established Church of Scotland, protesting against Government interference, left the Established Church of Scotland and formed the 'Free Church'.

In a Highland parish, the Established Church minister, feeling guilty that parishioners had to walk six miles every Sunday to go to church, built a small Chapel-at-Ease at the other end of the parish, on a brae eight feet above the road. A week before it was opened, he asked a day labourer (poor as a church mouse) to construct a track from road to church door. The day labourer, pleased to be offered three days' pay, asked:

"Is this an Established Church or a Free Church you are building?"

The minister replied: "Oh, it is an Established Church."

"Well," replied the labourer, "I may be a poor man, but I will never build a track to help anyone to get into the Established Church," and he put his coat on again.

"Wait a minute," said the minister, "keep your coat off and come up the brae with me now to the church door."

When they got there the minister said:

"Now you build the road *down*: that will help people to get *out* of the Church of Scotland."

(That road can still be seen today.)

General Sir Gordon MacMillan of MacMillan, K.C.B., K.C.V.O., C.B.E., D.S.O., M.C., LL.D.,
Governor of Gibraltar, 1952–55; Late Argyll and Sutherland Highlanders.

When I was commanding the 15th Scottish Division, the Prime Minister, Mr. Winston Churchill, very kindly came to visit us shortly before we moved to our concentration area for the invasion of Normandy in 1944.

I paraded the 6th Battalion Royal Scots Fusiliers for his inspection, as he had commanded their predecessors in France during the 1914–18 war.

After this was over, the troops gathered round informally while Winston Churchill mounted a platform to address them.

Somewhat to everyone's surprise, he looked at them rather sternly and then said in a ferocious tone of voice:

"There is only one thing wrong with Scotsmen…" Then came a pause while we all wondered what enormity we had committed. Much to everyone's relief the end of the sentence was, "…there are not enough of them."

The Late Brigadier John F. Macnab, C.B.E., D.S.O.,
Representer of House of Barravorich in Clan Macnab.

Whilst on secondment to a Battalion of the King's African Rifles a young subaltern arrived from home to join us. He arrived just in time for lunch and as we sat down for the meal his neighbour ventured the remark:

"You are in the Norfolk Regiment, aren't you?" To which the young man replied, with his nose rather in the air:

"Yes, The Royal Norfolk Regiment."

There was a pause of some ten seconds when the Signals Officer, not noted for being talkative, coughed apologetically and said:

"I say, do you mind passing the Royal Worcestershire Sauce?"

**Major-General John M. McNeill, C.B., C.B.E.,
Principal Staff Officer to Secretary of State for Commonwealth Relations,
1964–74.**

Speaker to audience: "This is going to take a long time. I don't mind you looking at your watches but if you begin to shake them you will have me worried."

**Sir Patrick Macrory,
Formerly a Director of Unilever and the Bank of Ireland.**

A jeweller's shop in Dublin was robbed in broad daylight and Pat, an eye-witness, rushed to the police station panting with excitement.

"I saw it all," he said, "and, man, ye'll never believe it! There was this damned great elephant comes lumbering down Grafton Street, smashes the window with his tusks, puts in his trunk, scoops out all the jewels and away he goes."

"Boys, oh boys!" said the sergeant, "I've never heard the like of that. Was he an Indian elephant or an African elephant?"

"How do ye tell the difference?" asked Pat.

"Well, you see," said the sergeant, "an Indian elephant has wee small ears which he keeps close to his head, but an African elephant has great big floppy ears which stick out. Which sort of ears did this fella have?"

"Oh, I couldn't tell ye that," said Pat, "sure, wasn't he wearing a stocking mask!"

**Magnus Magnusson, F.R.S.E.,
Writer and Broadcaster.**

News has just arrived from the Sinai desert of an archaeological excavation which has been interpreted as evidence of the earliest recorded Hebrew suicide. It was a grave, in which the skeleton had a knife still protruding from between the fourth and fifth ribs, and the fingers of the right hand still clasped round it.

In the fingers of the left hand there was a small piece of papyrus. On it was written:

"50,000 shekels on Goliath."

Sir George Mahon, Bt.

Some years ago when I was living in the country I went to Dublin for the day. The car broke down and I was landed in Dublin for the night without any luggage. I went to the Kildare Street Club which I had just joined, and told the hall porter of my predicament. He said I could have a bedroom, so I went and had some dinner and eventually went up to bed. To my delight when I opened the bedroom door I found a red silk dressing gown hanging on the door, pyjamas, slippers, razor, sponge and a toothbrush, all provided! The next morning I congratulated the valet on this and asked him how he had achieved it.

"Well, sir, I'll tell you the way it was. Poor General Jones died in the Club last week!"

Air Vice-Marshal Aleksander Maisner, C.B., C.B.E., A.F.C., Assistant Commandant, Royal Air Force College, Cranwell, 1971–73.

As someone who had to learn English from scratch rather late in life and yet do a fair amount of public speaking, I have always been very conscious of the vagaries of the English language and of its idiom lest it should lead to misunderstanding. Indeed, how can one avoid being misunderstood when:

Oversight can mean observation or the lack of it; *a dike* can be a ditch or a mound; *to cleave* can mean to stick together or to split apart; *fast* — fixed or moving at speed; *passive* and *impassive* are synonyms, as are *valuable* and *invaluable*; *shameless* is *shameful*, *flammable* is *inflammable*; to say '*I cannot help it*' means '*I cannot hinder it*'; *a cow in calf* is *a calf in cow*; to send '*a plum pudding to a young shaver at a public school*' is to send a pudding *without* plums to a youngster *who does not shave,* attending a school which *is not public*; and to find, on visiting someone in the morning, that '*he is not up yet*' and '*he is not down yet*', mean one and the same thing!

Lieut.-Colonel Arthur W.A. Malcolm, C.V.O.,
Queen's Foreign Service Messenger, 1955–68.

Many years ago when I was a very young officer we had a most charming Company Commander. Unfortunately, he was also rather deaf and somewhat easy-going. We also had an extremely efficient if somewhat intolerant Company Sergeant Major.

One day one of the less distinguished members of the Company was marched in front of the Company Commander on a minor charge. After the usual excuses the Company Commander turned to the C.S.M. and asked him what the man had said.

"Thank you, sir, for leave to speak," replied the C.S.M.

"He says he's a dirty idle man and deserves three drills. Right turn — quick march!"

Major-General Christopher M.M. Man, C.B., O.B.E., M.C. (Retired).

While I was President of the Regular Commissions Board at Westbury, whose task it was to select officers for the British Army, I received a letter from Field Marshal Montgomery inviting himself to the Establishment to watch the selection procedure.

The day arrived, and the great man appeared, dressed in blue uniform, with row upon row of medal ribbons. After watching the candidates at work under test, he was taken by me to see the accommodation provided for them. This consisted of a large hut, highly polished and well equipped, presided over by a civilian batman, an ex-serviceman. When the Field Marshal arrived at the door, there waiting for him was the batman in civilian clothes, flanked by the Quartermaster, an imposing figure in the

Scots Guards. The Field Marshal stopped in front of the batman and asked:

"Were you in the last war?"

The batman, who was almost overcome by being addressed by such a famous person, replied:

"Yes, sir, were you?"

We were aghast and waited for the Field Marshal's reply, which came after a short pause.

"Yes," he said, and burst out laughing.

The Late Sir Henry Mance,
Formerly, Chairman of Lloyd's.

There was once a very elderly professor who always had his shoes hand made. He went one day to his shoemaker and asked to see the leathers from which his next pair were to be made. He went through sample after sample and rejected piece after piece as being of inadequate quality. At length, the shoemaker got tired and said to the elderly professor:

"If I may suggest, sir, any of these leathers is likely to outlast you."

To which the professor replied, drawing himself up to his full height:

"I may well be over 90 but I can tell you that statistically it is a fact that very few people die after that age."

Lord Mancroft, K.B.E., T.D.,
Chairman, British Greyhound Racing Board.

All of us remember Nelson's signal at Trafalgar, "England expects that every man this day will do his duty", but not everyone remembers the reply of Admiral Lord Collingwood when he was handed the message on the quarterdeck of H.M.S. *Royal Sovereign*:

"I wish to God Nelson would stop sending us those damnfool signals," he said, rather testily. "We all know perfectly well what we have to do today."

All the same, I wish to God more of us knew perfectly well what we have to do today.

Professor Sir William Mansfield Cooper,
Vice-Chancellor, University of Manchester, 1956–70.

There are legions of academic stories but in my view one of the best, not too remote in time, relates to the University of Liverpool on an occasion when both Sir Winston Churchill and Sir Stafford Cripps were to receive honorary degrees.

The academic procession had been made ready, with the visiting dignitaries in their allotted places when, almost at the moment of departure, Sir Stafford asked whether he might have a drink of water. A porter was dispatched instantly with instructions that he was to lose no time. He quickly returned but in the rush of the moment proffered the water not to Sir Stafford but to Sir Winston. The old man's face clouded.

"Is this," he demanded, "compulsory?"

The Earl of March and Kinrara, D.L.

In 1956 I was doing a small administrative job at a conference in Oxford. I was told to meet a lorry which would be coming with some important equipment early the next morning. At 6 a.m. I was standing outside Tom Tower at Christ Church, when a lorry drew up with the equipment on board.

"Good morning," I said to the driver: "If you will take the first right and first right again you will come to another entrance close to the conference rooms where I will meet you."

"Hold on, governor," he said. "Who are you?"

"I am," I replied, very hesitatingly, "the er-er-er Earl of March."

"In that case," he replied, "I'm the Earl of April!"

Sir James Marjoribanks, K.C.M.G.,
Director, Scottish Council (Development and Industry) and Chairman,
E.E.C. Committee, since 1971.

A little, old, wrinkled, sharp Irish woman appeared before Lord Meadowbank as a witness in a murder case.

His Lordship's plea for greater clearness in her testimony was met with:

"Aye, Me Lord, but I canna' make it any clearer; for, Me Lord, I'm no schollard but just an old wife like yourself."

Sir Robert Mark, G.B.E., Q.P.M., Metropolitan Police Commissioner, 1972–77.

A friend of mine went last year to an insurance convention at a hotel in the United States. He was to speak at the convention dinner and on unpacking his dinner jacket found that his wife had only included a double-ended black tie. She always tied it for him when at home. If away he wore a ready-made one.

It was late, the shops were shut. He desperately tried to tie the wretched thing without success. Finally, he knocked on the door of the next bedroom and asked the occupant for help.

"Oh, sure!" he said, "but you'll have to lie on the bed face up." With sinking heart and much suspicion my friend did so. The tie was beautifully tied in about five seconds. As he thanked his saviour my friend said:

"But why did you want me to lie on the bed?"

To which came the slightly embarrassed reply: "Well, you see, I'm a mortician by profession."

Judge John Fitzgerald Marnan, M.B.E., Q.C., A Circuit Judge at the Old Bailey, 1972–80.

Sir Alan Herbert, known to many as 'A.P.H.', of *Punch*, belonged to a famous London dining club, of which many of the members were also, as he had been, Members of Parliament. There is a large club table and the conversation is frequently general.

On one occasion I was sitting near him while the talk ranged over the desirability, or otherwise, of having the provisions of a certain contentious Bill submitted to a Committee of the whole House. Someone suggested that, if not, this would be a bad instance of 'Thunderbolt Legislation' and added: "What do you think, Alan?"

The answer came: "Well, you may be right. I often think it is a pity that God did not have a committee stage before he drafted the Ten Commandments."

Sir Ralph Marnham, K.C.V.O., M.Chir., F.R.C.S.,
Serjeant Surgeon to The Queen, 1967–71.

In the flurry of activity which preceded the opening of the Festival of Britain, there were various delays. It was discovered that there was a shortage of shovels. An urgent request was sent to the Ministry of Works for more. The reply came back:

"Regret supply of shovels exhausted. Tell the men to lean on each other."

Sir Alan Marre, K.C.B.,
Formerly Parliamentary Commissioner for Administration (Ombudsman).

After Beethoven's death, a pupil of Rossini wrote a Requiem to commemorate the event, and took it to Rossini inviting his approval. After studying the composition, Rossini commented:

"What a pity it wasn't you who died and Beethoven who wrote the Requiem!"

Professor David C. Marsh,
Professor of Applied Social Science, University of Nottingham.

A highly motivated young lady had recently completed her course of training as a primary school teacher and took up her first appointment at a new progressive school.

On her first day she had been thrilled by the rapport she had established with her young pupils and in the last half hour before the school day ended she decided to experiment with the progressive methods of education which she had been taught, and encouraged the children to search for knowledge themselves.

"Let us," she said, "for the last half hour explore the world we live in."

The children readily agreed and in the last couple of minutes before the bell rang to end the day one youngster, Johnnie Smith, said:

"Excuse me, miss, but what is the weight of the world?"

Neither her major course in Geography at the College of Education nor indeed her extra year specialising for her Bachelor of Education degree, had provided the answer to this simple problem. However, not for nothing had she persevered with all the 'education modules' presented to her during her four years' training, so she said:

"Now that is a good question, Johnnie, and I suggest all of you should call in at the library on your way home and see if you can find out the weight of the world."

The bell rang, off the children went, and the young teacher dashed off to the main library in the city and mercifully found the answer.

First thing next morning, after assembly, she faced her class and said:

"Well, who found the answer to Johnnie's question?"

Not a single response; so feeling very confident, she said:

"Well, it was a very difficult question for you but the answer is 5,887,613,230,000,000,000,000 tons."

Still no response, except that Johnnie, who had asked the original question, put up his hand and said:

"Please, miss, is that with or without people?"

Major-General Roger S. Marshall, C.B., T.D., Director of Army Legal Services, 1971–73.

In 1829 some Irish had emigrated to a West Indian colony. The Negroes soon learnt their brogue, and when another shipload of Irish arrived soon afterwards, the Negroes called out:

"Ah, Paddy, how are ye?"

"Oh, Christ," said one of the new arrivals, "what, y're become black already!"

General Sir James Marshall-Cornwall, K.C.B., C.B.E., D.S.O., M.C., President, Royal Geographical Society, 1954–58.

At a dinner party in London the American Ambassador was asked by his lady table companion:

"Mr. Choate, what do you think is the most wonderful thing in the world?"

He replied:

"A beautiful woman."

"How dull!" said his neighbour. "I have always thought that *sleep* is."

"Well," said the American, "perhaps it is... *next* to a beautiful woman."

Major-General Peter Lawrence de Carteret Martin, C.B.E., Formerly Colonel 22nd (Cheshire) Regiment; Director of Personal Services (Army), 1971–74.

I was told this story by the C.O. 2nd Battalion The Parachute Regiment when I visited him on the island of Anguilla, and told it myself at a Regimental Dinner in the presence of our Colonel-in-Chief, H.R.H. The Prince of Wales, Earl of Chester, who is also Colonel-in-Chief of The Parachute Regiment.

When 2 Para landed in Anguilla to put down the alleged armed insurrection, they encountered no resistance and were generally welcomed. This was clearly a disappointment to the world media, which was there in strength, and a small number of them therefore persuaded some Anguillan bystanders to stage a 'demonstration' for the benefit of their cameramen.

This was all watched with disgust by the C.O.'s driver and radio operator, seated nearby in their Land Rover. At the end of the 'demonstration' a man carrying a tape-recorder walked across to the driver, thrust a microphone in front of him and said:

"You lika to say something for Radio Italia?"

With a completely poker face the driver took the microphone, put it to his lips, and said: "Two ice-creams please."

I struck up a conversation with the taxi-driver taking me to Euston, en route to Chester where I was to preside at our Annual Regimental Dinner. He told me he had served with our Training Battalion for a short time during the Second World War.

"The C.O. was a proper bastard," he said.

"In what way?" I asked.

"Well, I'll give you a for instance. One day I am on sentry duty outside the Guard Room when I see the colonel approaching on his bicycle. I shout, 'Turn out the Guard!' and the guard doubles out beside me. As the C.O. comes level with us the corporal gives, 'Present Arms'. The C.O. says 'Very smart, corporal', takes his hand off the handlebars to salute, and falls off. The corporal runs forward to pick him up — and the colonel puts him under close arrest for leaving his post."

I told the story that night at the Regimental Dinner and no one was more delighted than the veteran Colonel 'X' himself.

**Judge Peter Mason, Q.C.,
Senior Circuit Judge, Snaresbrook Crown Court.**

Sometimes jurors get one up on the judge. There was an occasion when a juror, a young man, turned up a day late for jury service. I asked him why he had not appeared on the previous day, to which his reply was:

"Me mum got burnt."

"Oh dear," I said, "I am sorry. Not badly, I hope?"

"Aw yes," he replied, "they don't mess about at Wood Green Crematorium."

The Rt. Hon. Roy Mason, M.P.,
Formerly Secretary of State, Northern Ireland.

On arriving at Doncaster railway station to catch my train to London I found the platform unusually crowded and indeed, on boarding the train, could not find a first-class seat. I therefore toured the second class — all were full except one compartment which was reserved for patients from one of the local mental institutions. It was empty, the train was about to depart, so I took a seat.

However, just as the train pulled away the party arrived and started filling the seats. Of course, one person was left standing. The organiser immediately said:

"We had better have a count...one, two, three...who are you?" he said, pointing at me.

"Oh, I'm Roy Mason, M.P. for Barnsley"..."four, five..."

Viscount Massereene and Ferrard, D.L.,
President, Charitable and other Organisations.

My paternal grandfather came out of White's Club, St. James's Street, one night and was perceived by a policeman who noticed that he was walking in a very erratic manner. The constable asked if anything was the matter and whether he could be of any assistance. My grandfather replied:

"No, no, it's quite all right, it's only Massereene and Ferrard, both very drunk."

The same relative was in a great hurry one day to get from Belfast to the town of Antrim, where his Northern Ireland residence, Antrim Castle, was situated. Rushing up the Belfast Station platform he jumped onto the engine and prevailed upon the driver to let him take over, to which request the driver acquiesced, no doubt with the help of a sovereign or two. My grandfather promptly drove the train in record time to Antrim. He forgot, however, to stop at the intermediate stations, with the result that he gave a guinea to any passenger thus inconvenienced.

It turned out to be a very expensive journey!

When my mother was engaged to my father they were coming back from hunting one evening in Co. Louth, Ireland. It was dark with a light rain falling. They were driving along a long narrow country lane when my mother suddenly said:

"Be careful of that man on a grey horse just ahead."

My father could see no one. My mother then shouted:

"Look out, you're nearly on him."

My father, who still could not see any horse or rider, jammed on the brakes.

"It's all right now," my mother interjected, "he's gone down that lane to the left." She then remarked on his odd appearance: long hair tied at the back, riding boots that folded over at the top, and a long skirted blue coat.

Some months later when my mother was married and installed at Antrim Castle she entered a room and instantly recognised the subject of the portrait opposite as being the man she had seen that wet winter's night turn down the lane in front of the headlights. Research in the castle library subsequently brought to light that he was an 18th century member of the family, who had owned the land where they had been driving and where he turned down the lane was the western boundary of the estate.

Professor Denis Matthews, C.B.E.,
Professor of Music, University of Newcastle upon Tyne.

A cellist was heard practising for hours on the balcony of a hotel in Istanbul. He played, however, only one note though with all manner of bowings, sometimes long, sometimes short, spiccato, pizzicato, and all the rest. An Englishman who overheard him and met him later in the bar mentioned that all other cellists he knew moved the left hand as well as the right hand and played many different notes, tunes, in fact.

"Ah!" the one-note player replied, "*they* are still looking for it — *I've found it!*"

Professor Geoffrey Matthews,
Emeritus Professor of Mathematics Education, University of London.

Tommy: "Hurry up and finish your dinner, Grandma."
Grandma: "Why?"
Tommy: "Dad says I can have a bike when you've had your chips."

Professor Leonard Maunder, O.B.E.,
Professor of Mechanical Engineering, University of Newcastle upon Tyne.

Sometimes people catch the wrong trains.

Shortly before an Edinburgh express approached York a rather small passenger named Brown confided to the only other occupant of his compartment, MacDonald, that he had some business to conduct at York and was pleased the train was arriving early.

"Too bad," said MacDonald, "the train doesn't stop at York."

After various possibilities had been considered and discarded, a plan of action was agreed. MacDonald would lower Brown from an open window as the train passed slowly through York station and, in order to improve his chances of staying upright on landing, Brown would wave his legs suitably during his descent.

All went well at first. Brown's legs thrashed the air, he landed well, shot down the platform, side-stepping the while to avoid stationary objects, and was slowing up satisfactorily when the guard's van of the accelerating train caught up with him. The burly Scottish guard did not hesitate. Reaching out, he gripped the runner firmly around the waist and, as he hauled him back on the train, shouted admiringly:

"Weel done, laddie, yer nearly missed it!"

Sir Peter Medawar, O.M., C.H., C.B.E., F.R.S.,
Medical Scientist; Nobel Prize for Medicine, 1960.

Three Swiss businessmen died and when they reached heaven they asked for an interview with God. When God received them, their spokesman said, with great reverence and humility:

"O Lord, we sought an audience of You to express our profound gratitude for having been privileged to spend our mortal lives in the most beautiful country in the world: our glorious lakes and towering mountains and serene pasturelands have no equal in the whole world.

"As a mark of our gratitude we lay before You a characteristic product of our homeland."

So saying, they laid at God's feet a huge Emmenthaler cheese.

An uneasy silence followed: the three Swiss shuffled their feet and exchanged uneasy glances.

"Thank you, my children," said God, observing their unease. "Did you wish to address Me further?"

"Why, yes, Almighty," said their spokesman boldly, "that will be 400 francs."

Rt. Hon. Sir Robert Megarry,
The Vice-Chancellor, High Court of Justice.

The statute book is usually thought to be both dull and obscure. It does indeed lack literary charm. Thus no verse is to be found in it, even though a rhyme has been suggested which might suitably be inserted in almost any modern Act of Parliament:

'If anything shall seem,
The Minister may deem;
His certificate of demption
Shall confer complete exemption'.

Yet consolation for this lack of verse is to be found in some brilliant flights of fancy: Parliament can indeed do anything. Consider, for example, the war-time power that was given to the Minister of Agriculture to make an order 'prohibiting or restricting the movement of bees'; the poor immobilised law-abiding bees! But perhaps the happiest concept of all is that enshrined in section 468, sub-section (10), of the Income Tax Act, 1952, no less. This dealt with limited companies and the like; and it provided that 'a body corporate shall not be deemed to cease to be resident in the United Kingdom by reason only that it ceases to exist'.

Air Chief Marshal Sir Walter Merton, G.B.E., K.C.B., Air A.D.C. to the Queen, 1962–63.

American friends have been much amused by an incident which took place in 1943 when I was the Group Captain commanding Royal Air Force Station Luqa in Malta.

It was my responsibility to allocate any passengers or freight to aircraft passing through Malta. At that time there was an American general who wished to be flown to North Africa. The same evening a U.S.A.F. Dakota, captained by a very tall lean Texan, happened to be night-stopping at Luqa so it was arranged that he should take on the American general. As the general wanted an early take-off I instructed that the crew sleep on the station rather than in one of our messes accommodated in requisitioned hotels in Sliema.

I was on the airfield early to meet and see off the general.

To my surprise and irritation I found that the aircraft was not ready and the crew nowhere to be found on the station.

Apologising to the general I sent a car to fetch the crew from Sliema and instructed that they report to me on arrival.

When the crew arrived they marched up to me and the tall gum-chewing Texan gave me a curt salute and said:

"Good morning, Cap'n."

I asked whether he had received my orders to sleep on the station, to which he replied:

"Sure, but we wanted to see Sliema."

I then made it clear that when he was at Luqa he must comply with my instructions.

Gazing hard at me he said:

"Say — this is an American (pronounced Mericun) ship."

I then firmly pointed out that this was an R.A.F. Station and that he

either obey my orders or never come
back again. Looking down at me,
as I am not tall, he retorted:

"Say — suits me."

I could do nothing but laugh, and
so ended the interview — the
Texan clearly coming off best!

**Sir Anthony Meyer, Bt., M.P.,
Former Diplomat.**

The late, much beloved, Pope John XXIII, before he became Pope,
served for a period as Papal Nuncio in Paris. As such he was involved in the
diplomatic scene in that elegant city and had to attend a number of social
functions of a distinctly worldly character. Somebody asked him whether
this was a source of distress to him in any way.

"On the contrary," he replied, "I enjoy it very much. The only thing is,
that when a lady comes to dinner in a dress that is cut a little too tight
behind or a little too low in front, everyone looks, not at her, but at me."

Cliff Michelmore, C.B.E.,
Television Broadcaster and Producer.

I think that I shall never see
A hazard tougher than a tree —
A tree o'er which my ball must fly
If on the green it is to lie;
A tree which stands that green to guard,
And makes the shot extremely hard;
A tree whose leafy arms extend
To kill the three-wood shot I send;
A tree that stands in silence there
While angry golfers rave and swear.
Wedges were made for fools like me,
Who cannot even miss a tree.

Sir George Middleton, K.C.M.G., F.R.S.A.,
Diplomat; H.M. Ambassador to the United Arab Republic, 1964–66.

Elderly Englishman: "I have very simple tastes. Give me a bottle of whisky, a tin of biscuits and a dog and I'm perfectly happy."
"Why the dog?" asked his friend.
"Well, someone's got to eat the biscuits!" he replied.

"It's so exciting that you're now married and all!" chirruped one young lady. "Have you told your family and all your other friends?"
"No," said the second girl, "I'm waiting for my husband to sober up. I think it's only right that he should be the first to know the news."

"I'm a man of strict principles," said the man at the club. "For example, I never slept with my wife until after we were married; I wonder whether you can say as much?"
"Let me see," said the other member, "what was your wife's maiden name?"

Adam and Eve used to walk about in the Garden of Eden. One day God said to Adam:

"When you walk with Eve, I want you to go hand-in-hand."

"What does hand-in-hand mean?" asked Adam, and an angel explained it to him.

A little later God said:

"That is very good, but now you should walk with your arm around Eve's waist."

"What is a waist?" asked Adam, and the angel told him. Later again Adam was told that he should now kiss Eve from time to time during their walks.

"What is a kiss?" asked Adam, and the same obliging angel had to show how it was done.

So the day came when God said:

"Splendid, my children! Now go forth and multiply and replenish the earth!"

But next morning Adam was back again.

"What is a headache?" he asked.

Ian Mikardo, M.P.,
Member of Parliament for Bethnal Green and Bow.

There is, it is said, a noted physician in Moscow who has received a special award for being the leading Stakhanovite in the medical profession in the U.S.S.R. One morning he rushed into a major hospital to do his rounds and said to the matron:

"I'm terribly behind my schedule this morning, and in an awful hurry, so just tell me the average temperature of all the patients in all my wards."

Sir Richard Miller,
Chairman, Arthritis and Rheumatism Council, North-West Region.

Doctor (on telephone to local plumber):
"The kitchen sink is stopped up and it is
most inconvenient. Will you come round
and deal with it immediately?"

Plumber: "It's after 6 p.m. and all my
men have gone home. I can't do anything
until the morning."

Doctor: "Can't you come yourself?"

Plumber: "No, I am going out shortly."

Doctor: "In our profession you know, we turn
out morning, noon or night if someone is in trouble."

Plumber: "All right, doctor, I'll be round soon."

The plumber duly arrives, looks at the sink, removes a bottle of aspirins
from his pocket and throws the tablets into the sink, and then says to the
doctor:

"Well, we'll see how it goes on and I'll be back in the morning."

Vice-Admiral Sir Charles P. Mills, K.C.B., C.B.E., D.S.C.,
Commander-in-Chief Plymouth, 1967–69; Lieutenant-Governor and C-in-C
Guernsey, 1969–74.

When Admiral Lord Mountbatten was making his film series for
Granada TV, I entertained him to lunch in my flagship, *Victorious*, at
Singapore. The sweet course was rum omelette, which I believe was one of
the Admiral's favourites. He remarked on its excellence and I told him that
my Chinese cook had spent some two-and-a-half hours whipping it by
hand that morning.

After lunch the Admiral asked to see
the cook, whose English was not
very good and who was accustomed to
being asked how long he had been in
the Navy. When the Admiral asked
how long he had spent making the
omelette, the cook answered:

"Sixteen years."

Lord Mishcon,
Lawyer.

The occasion was a luncheon in honour of two munificent patrons of music (in fact, a twin brother and sister) on their seventieth birthdays, at which I found that I was the third in a list of four speakers—the other three being very distinguished personalities in the artistic world.

Just before it was my turn to speak I turned to my luncheon neighbour who happened to be the well-known pianist, Gina Bachauer, and casually asked, in the hope of getting some inspiration:

"What would you say is the purpose of the *third* movement in a symphony?"

To my delight she innocently replied:

"How funny you should ask that. Frankly, I have always thought that the third movement served little or no purpose except perhaps to show by contrast how good the *other* movements are."

The dear lady nearly collapsed when I immediately rose and told the story to my audience.

Sir Derek Mitchell, K.C.B., C.V.O.,
Director, Standard Chartered Bank.

A hunter was out with his gun. As he approached a wood a girl ran out with no clothes on. The hunter said:

"Are you game?"

The girl said:

"Yes."

So he shot her.

Professor George A.G. Mitchell, O.B.E., T.D.,
Emeritus Professor of Anatomy, Manchester University.

The late Lord Stopford, when Vice-Chancellor of Manchester University, was once asked by the secretary of the local Rotary Club if he would nominate one of his professors to give an after-luncheon talk. Stopford agreed to do so, but asked for suggestions about a preferred topic, as this would help him in making a selection.

The secretary stated that the subject was unimportant, provided the speaker was witty. The V.C. replied that he had no wits amongst his professors, but that he could easily supply two half-wits.

The Hon. Sir Alan Mocatta, O.B.E.,
A High Court Judge.

A young man was just back from his first visit to Israel. When asked how he liked it, he said:

"It was splendid. We saw the whole country from Dan to Beer Sheba. Do you know I always thought they were husband and wife — just like Sodom and Gomorrah."

One woman talking to another:
"I always take two hot water bottles to bed — in case one leaks."

**Rear-Admiral Anthony J. Monk, C.B.E.,
Rear-Admiral Engineering, Naval Air Command, 1976–78; Director-General,
Brick Development Association.**

After some years in the Fleet Air Arm I returned to sea in H.M.S. *Apollo* and had a lot of fun in what was then the Navy's fastest major warship. A ship of the same class, *Manxman* — which was often in company with *King George V* in the Pacific — was the subject of an incident when she joined the U.S. 7th Fleet. The U.S. Fleet Commander, taking pity on the elderly three-funnelled ship, reduced the speed of the Fleet to 25 knots. To his surprise, *Manxman* remained in station and so he increased speed to 30 knots. *Manxman* kept up without apparent difficulty so a signal was sent:

"Speed of the Fleet 35 knots; *Manxman* make best speed." A short while later *Manxman,* at 40 knots, was fast disappearing ahead of the Fleet signalling "Why?".

The effect of extreme heat sometimes placed on sailors in a ship reminds me of the story of the boy seaman who wrote home from his training establishment:

"Dear Mum, I have just been moved to a new bed. I have a bedside light and a colour telly. I can get up and go to bed when I want to, and there's a pretty girl who brings me an early morning cup of tea.

P.S. I also have measles.

A change for the better which took place during my service was the admission of the fairer sex to mess dinners, but this did inhibit the range of one's after-dinner stories. One I found suited to such occasions was about the very young lady who was sent up to put herself to bed because her parents were giving a very important dinner party. In the middle of dinner the door opened and the very young lady appeared stark naked and clutching a dripping wet nightdress.

Marching up to the important gentlemen guests, she pointed an accusing finger at each in turn and said:

"You, or you, or you, left the seat up — and I fell in."

Sir Leslie Monson, K.C.M.G., C.B.,
Formerly Deputy Under-Secretary of State, Foreign and Commonwealth Office.

In the early 'thirties, Dr. Lang, then Archbishop of Canterbury, attended a dinner at Balliol College where he had been an undergraduate after having been at Glasgow University. He had connections with two other Oxford colleges; All Souls, of which he had been elected a Fellow, and Magdalen, of which the Archbishop of Canterbury is Visitor.

In his after-dinner speech, he said rather pompously:

"Balliol was my mother, All Souls was my nurse and, though it is perhaps something an archbishop should not say, Magdalen was my mistress."

At this point a voice, with a Scottish accent, came from the back of the hall:

"Aye, and Glasgow was your pre-natal clinic."

The Hon. Ewen Montagu, C.B.E., Q.C., D.L.,
Chairman of Middlesex Sessions; Judge Advocate of the Fleet, 1945–73.

A speech need not be long to be good — indeed, the shorter the better. The shortest and most effective speech ever made in a murder trial was, in its entirety, as follows:

"Gentlemen of the jury. If you convict my client she will be taken from here to a cold damp cell in Sing Sing prison. There all of her lovely blonde hair will be shaved off, she will be strapped to a chair and burnt to a cinder.

"But, gentlemen of the jury, if you acquit her, she will return to her luxurious apartment, the telephone number of which is Rhinelander 0123."

Colonel Frank S. Morgan, C.B.E., E.R.D., D.L., J.P.,
Hon. Colonel, 50 and 81 A.F. Signal Regiments, 1952–60.

This story goes back to 1917 when the British Forces in Egypt under General Allenby were waiting for the big advance into Palestine. The Imperial Camel Brigade, which consisted of three Battalions of mixed British, Australian and New Zealand troops, was in camp some miles south of El Arish, with nothing on their flank except the Sinai Desert. I was Brigade Signal Officer and when the general came back from his morning inspection he asked me if there were any messages from G.H.Q. I handed him a message which described a certain German spy who was supposed to be in our area.

The general read it and said:

"That must have been the fellow I met at 3rd Battalion H.Q. He seemed to be rather inquisitive but explained that he was an Engineer Officer looking for suitable sites for advanced ammunition dumps."

The message described the spy as speaking excellent English, usually armed, and a first-class shot, and absolutely ruthless. When the general had read it he said:

"Lucky we did not see this before we went out, as otherwise I might have done something reckless, but he is probably back in the Turkish lines by now."

As the general himself had previously won both the Military Cross and the Victoria Cross, the chances of doing something reckless were pretty great! Or perhaps it was just as well that the spy had already left.

Some time in 1945 I was a senior staff officer of sufficient weight to get a staff car and even an aeroplane when necessary. While waiting for a car to take me from Jerusalem to Lydda (where I could pick up a plane) I was approached by an officer who said:

"Sir, could you offer a lady a lift to Cairo?"

"That depends on the lady," I replied.

"It is the one sitting over there in the corner," he said.

After a glance I said:

"Certainly," and we set off for Lydda.

We discovered a mutual language — French — and chatted away until we got to Lydda. At this point I had to produce my official pass and the duty officer asked:

"Is this lady your wife?"

I replied, unthinkingly, in English:

"Good God, no!"

Then to my complete embarrassment she said:

"I speaka a leetle English, yes!" and it took me the rest of the trip across Sinai to apologise adequately.

The Earl of Morley,
Farmer and Company Director.

The chairman at a dinner introduced the principal speaker as, "A pillar of the Church and a column in the *News of the World*."

Air Vice-Marshal Ronald J.A. Morris, C.B. (Retired).

An elderly Scots lady of strict Presbyterian upbringing, was returning from a visit to her daughter in France and had to spend a night in Paris before getting the early morning train next day.

She spent the night in a small but very respectable hotel off the Champs Elysées. Having had dinner and packed her luggage ready for an early start next morning she retired to bed. Just as she was about to drop off to sleep she became aware of a strange, irritating noise which she eventually identified as loud snores coming through the wall from the next room.

She stood this as long as possible but, realising that as long as the snoring persisted, sleep for her would not come, she rose and knocked on the wall, whereupon the noise immediately ceased.

She got back into bed and once again was about to drop off when the dreaded snoring restarted. At first, she did her best to ignore it, but the more she tried the worse it seemed to become until she was forced once more to bang on the wall with her fist, which produced the desired result.

Unfortunately, the cure was not permanent, but once more she decided to try to ignore it, even going to the length of putting her head under the blankets — but still sleep would not come. At last, in desperation, she leant out of bed, seized her leather-soled slipper and banged it furiously on the wall. Again the snoring ceased, but then to her utter horror, she heard a muffled Scots voice coming through the wall saying:

"Aye, it's all right my lass, you can knock away but I'm no' comin' through."

Acutely embarrassed, the lady slept a little that night and left *very* early next morning before the other guests appeared.

Professor Huw Morris-Jones,
Head of Department of Social Theory, University College of North Wales,
Bangor (Retired).

A memorial tablet in a church in Simla (India).

"Sacred to the memory of Brigadier Lancelot David Warnock of the Royal Hussars, who was accidentally killed by his batman on October 5th, 1872.

"Well done, thou good and faithful servant."

Lord Morrison of Tottenham,
Hon. President, Robert Browning Settlement,
from 1967.

We say we have sex equality in this country yet why is it that a Peer's wife is known as a Lady and later on Dowager, whereas a Peeress's husband stays a Mr.?

Lords are famous people, for they are just like lunatics and criminals in that they are not allowed to vote at General Elections.

Sir Brian Morton, F.R.I.C.S.,
Chairman, Harland & Wolff (Shipbuilders), 1975–80.

My company decided to establish a pension scheme for the employees. It was a case of all or none. Everyone agreed except Sammy Smith, who, despite pressure from all his colleagues, refused to sign. Eventually they appealed to me, as chairman, to try to persuade Sammy Smith to sign.

I had one of those difficult and frustrating days and so when Sammy Smith arrived in my office I spoke somewhat irritably:

"Sammy, you know about this pension scheme, why the b—— h—— will you not sign when everyone else has signed?"

"I will sign," he said, and did so.

"Tell me, Sammy, why wouldn't you sign before, when all your mates, the foreman and shop steward, asked you to?"

Sammy replied: "None of them ever explained it to me as well as you did."

Captain The Lord Mottistone (R.N. Retired).

On peacekeeping operations in tropical waters about fifteen years ago, the ship I was commanding was acting in support of the Army up a narrow waterway. We anchored for the night. After receiving a report from my Army colleagues that an attack was possible, but most unlikely, I ordered a low degree of readiness for action and turned in.

At about two o'clock in the morning, an anxious officer of the watch reported the silhouette of a large ship on the port beam. Rushing onto the bridge, I saw indeed that there appeared to be a large strange ship close abeam. There was no time to waste, so I pressed the alarm bells for the ship's company to go to action stations.

Just as the reports of readiness for action started coming in the Army post on the river bank switched off its searchlight. Our adversary had disappeared! Our own ship had been silhouetted against the jungle foliage!

Air Vice-Marshal Leslie Moulton, C.B., D.F.C., A.O.C. No. 90 (Signals) Group R.A.F., 1969–71.

Hamish's first job took him south, all the way to London, where for the very first time he had to fend for himself. His doting parents had arranged for him to live in a block of bachelor flats but his mother was a little uneasy about him; so, some weeks later, she took the train from Inverness to see how her bonny lad was getting on.

"How do you like living here, Hamish?" she asked.

"Och it's fine, mam," he replied, "except for the neighbours: the idiot on this side keeps banging his head against the wall and the one on that side screams and yells awee inta the neet."

"How on earth do you stand it, laddie?" asked his mother. "What do you do while all this is going on?"

"Och, weel, I dinna do nuthin'," said young Hamish. "I just bide heerr quietly practising on ma bagpipes."

Viscount Mountgarret.

My father possessed a very good cellar which was well known amongst his circle of friends. When he was a comparatively young man he entertained a large dinner party after a day's hunting. The moment came when the port was to be served. Many people round the table were much older than he, and they too prided themselves on their knowledge and experience of the vintages of the various ports that might be offered. One of them, a fairly senior 'hunting man' was seen to be sniffing and perusing his port in a rather quizzical fashion. My father enquired of him if there was anything wrong, to which the man replied:

"I think this port is corked."

Whereat the other guests round the table all picked their glasses up, and sniffed and tasted, and all shook their heads and agreed with the 'senior citizen' that indeed the port was corked.

The butler had, by this time, retired from the room, and therefore had no knowledge of what had happened. My father called out to him:

"Jones, bring the other decanter of port, please."

The butler came with the second decanter, the glasses were cleared and fresh glasses were placed, and the new decanter was passed round.

"Ah," the hunting man said, "this is definitely superior to the first decanter."

Everybody nodded in agreement. My father said to the butler:

"Jones, which bottle of port is this?," to which the butler replied:

"It's the other half of the magnum, my Lord!"

Richard Murdoch,
Stage, Film, Radio and Television Actor.

The miserable looking man in the railway carriage was explaining his misfortunes to the other occupant.

"I've been to the races and on my way there I leant out of the carriage window and my hat blew away. It was a very expensive hat I had bought this very morning. I got to the races — still fed up about losing my hat — and then went and backed a loser in the first five races. So I decided that if there was a horse running in the last race whose name suggested a hat, I would back it. On looking through the race card the only horse with a name like a hat was 'Sunkissed'. I thought, 'I've got a bald head — sun kisses my head — makes my hair grow — hat', so I backed it."

"I take it the horse didn't win," said the other occupant.

"No, came in last. The race was won by some bloody horse called 'Mon Chapeau'."

Gordon Muir, F.R.I.C.S.,
Formerly a Baillie of the City of Glasgow.

Some years ago the Corporation of Glasgow promoted a mass chest X-ray campaign. To encourage public support it was decided that members of the Town Council would set an example and be the first to be examined.

A mobile unit was parked in George Square and in due course the councillors, suitably escorted by the press, emerged from the City Chambers with proper solemnity and made their way to the unit.

Sadly, history has failed to record the name of the passer-by who studied the distinguished procession and commented:

"It disna' take an X-ray to see through that lot."

In the days of its former glory, the Corporation of Glasgow met every second Thursday. An orchid was provided for each councillor, the magistrates wore their chains of office, and the whole was presided over by the Lord Provost, resplendent in a magnificent coat, white tie and wing collar.

True to the democratic principle, a small number of the public were permitted to view the proceedings. During a lull in a particularly acrimonious debate, a little old lady in the gallery was heard to comment:

"Ah kent this wus a circus, but they never tellt me you'd got a ringmaster."

Rear-Admiral William J. Munn, C.B., D.S.O., O.B.E., Formerly Chief of Staff to the Commander-in-Chief, Home Fleet.

In the summer of 1937 I was privileged to be appointed Flag Lieutenant to Vice-Admiral Sir Andrew Cunningham, who later became Admiral of the Fleet, Lord Cunningham of Hyndhope, but was then Admiral Commanding the Battle Cruiser Squadron in the Mediterranean and flying his flag in H.M.S. *Hood*.

Depending upon the ages of his many admirers he was known either as 'A.B.C.' or 'Uncle Ned.' Having no children of their own, he and Lady Cunningham surrounded themselves with real or adopted nephews and nieces and my sister, during part of this time, was one of the fortunate young women to stay with them in Malta.

One morning at breakfast in their flat, after a dinner party in *Hood* the previous evening, A.B.C. said he couldn't understand why the women took so long to powder their noses after dinner on board. They had taken 20 minutes last night. My sister (whose nickname was 'Bubbles') wasn't wearing this and rather cheekily replied:

"If your rotten little ship had more than one lavatory for the women they wouldn't take so long. As there were ten on board last night and they only took 20 minutes, two minutes each was not bad going."

A few days later there was another dinner party on board, including five admirals' wives and my sister. The admiral's barge was sent inshore at Malta to pick up the guests and they were all on time, except my sister, who had been to a party with some Maltese.

She arrived at the jetty to find a frantic admiral's coxswain just about to shove off without her and with some pretty impatient admirals' ladies.

When they got to *Hood* A.B.C. was standing at the top of the gangway ready to receive them, and my sister, being the lowest form of human life, a mere Flag Lieutenant's sister, came up the gangway last.

When she shook the admiral's hand she apologised profusely and said it was entirely her fault for being 10 minutes late. With that glorious twinkle in his eye he smiled and said:

"Only one minute each tonight, Bubbles."

The Late Lord Murray of Gravesend, Formerly Political Aide to Sir Harold Wilson.

On arriving at Gravesend station, I took a taxi to my home. The driver said to me:

"It's Mr. Brown, isn't it?" and I replied:

"No, it's Lord Murray."

His quick answer was:

"Oh, yes, I meant to say that!"

A man went to a doctor for a check-up. The doctor said:
"You should have come a lot earlier for a check-up. I am afraid I have some bad news for you. You have only three minutes to live."
The man was absolutely shattered and said:
"Doctor — is there nothing you can do at all?" and the doctor replied:
"Do you fancy a boiled egg?"

Sir Peter Mursell, M.B.E., D.L.,
Vice-Lord Lieutenant, West Sussex.

One day my wife went to have a bath, forgetting that the plumber was working in the loft and that the trap door was in the bathroom.
As she lay back she saw the gaping hole in the ceiling and to her horror a face appeared looking down.
The plumber, with immense tact, retired to the far end of the loft, murmuring:
"I'm sorry, sir!"

Sir Humphrey Mynors, Bt.,
Deputy Governor, Bank of England, 1954–64.

Travelling once by train from Leeds to Peterborough I forgot to change at Grantham into the following train and found myself non-stop to London.
My wife was meeting me at Peterborough. What to do? I told the steward in the breakfast car of my trouble. He produced a timetable, and pencil and paper to write a note; cut a cleft in a potato and stuffed the note into it.
As we ran through Peterborough he lobbed the potato to the feet of a porter. When my wife arrived a few minutes later the station staff were watching for her car number and told her which train to meet from London.
There was no charge, except the return fare from Peterborough to London.
Who says British Rail is lacking in initiative?

Sir Patrick Nairne, G.C.B., M.C.,
Permanent Secretary, Department of Health and Social Security, since 1975.

The story of a farmer and his horse carries a lesson for the permanent civil servant.

One spring the farmer rode round his acres and found a stream he was accustomed to fording deeper and most difficult to cross because of the winter rains. He and the horse had an unpleasant and rather alarming crossing through swirling waters. In the late summer the farmer rode that way again. Weeks of drought had almost dried up the ford; but, when the horse reached the edge of the shallow waters, it was most unwilling to cross. Eventually the farmer became impatient; he hit the horse with his stick and forced him to cross.

"Get on, you old fool," he shouted. "Your memory is better than your judgement."

Lord Napier of Magdala, O.B.E.,
Retired Brigadier, Late Royal Engineers.

The principal guest at a mess night in Chitral was an elderly councillor to His Highness The Mehtas who was a devout Muslim, a 'Pasha', as he had done a pilgrimage to Mecca. The dinner had gone well and the mess secretary was just congratulating himself when he realised that among the dessert being handed round was a dish of 'Tipsy Prunes' and the Pasha was about to eat them. Before he had time to say anything the Pasha ate one, so the mess secretary hoped he would not realise that he had taken some of the forbidden alcohol, and kept quiet.

When he had finished the prunes, the Pasha took out his handkerchief and carefully wrapped the stones in it and put it back in his pocket, to take them home to plant in his garden.

In the 1930s, King Amanullah of Afghanistan decided to do a royal tour of Europe. His route lay through Quetta and by the Viceroy's special train down the Bolan Pass.

Suddenly, in the middle of a tunnel, the emergency chain was pulled and the train came to a halt.

The anxious authorities rushed along the train to the royal coach, but no one had pulled the alarm chain.

Nobody admitted to having pulled the chain and an inspection eventually showed that the alarm chain had been pulled in the royal lavatory.

Amanullah or his Queen had obviously pulled the wrong chain!

Sir David Napley,
Past President of the Law Society.

When I organised the Law Society's Advocacy Training courses I included a talk on the psychology of the courts, since some understanding of the subject is vital in the conduct of any case.

On one occasion, at the conclusion of a lecture, an earnest young lawyer came diffidently to his feet.

"We have a client," he said, "who has some matrimonial trouble. Three of my partners and a legal executive have all had a go at her and she still denies that she has committed adultery. How can one tell whether or not a person is lying in these circumstances?"

The lecturing doctor paused for a moment, and then said:

"When a person is lying the saliva in their mouth dries up and they start to lick their lips; thus, if you see someone licking their lips in these circumstances it is a fair indication that they are probably lying."

Since then, I have carried out some research of my own. I find that whenever I mention adultery to any of my clients they all start licking their lips.

And that is not the end of it. Then, when I go into court and mention it to the judge, he starts licking his.

Major-General Sir John Nelson, K.C.V.O., C.B., D.S.O., O.B.E., M.C., Vice-President, National Playing Fields Association.

While driving, with my wife beside me and my two springer spaniels in the back of the car, I was involved in an accident, one of the direct results of which was that I was rendered unconscious.

On coming round while my head was being stitched up by an Indian doctor, I asked him:

"Are the dogs all right?"

"Oh, yes, the dogs they are very well."

"And my wife, is she all right?"

"Yes, your wife is fine."

When, two days later I was sufficiently recovered, the head of the hospital came to examine me. After he had finished he said:

"Do you know that the Indian doctor who stitched you up is absolutely delighted with you? He says that, at last, he has met a real British gentleman."

"Oh," I said, "how very nice, I wonder why."

"Because," the answer came, "you asked after your dogs before your wife!"

Lieut.-Colonel Sir Edmund Neville, Bt., M.C.,
Prime Warden, Fishmongers' Company, 1958–59.

This is a Norfolk story.

Amos Sparrow met George Flowerday at Acle market one day. Said Amos:

"George, boy, didn't you have a mare sick o' colic not long ago?"

George: "Oh, ah."

Amos: "What did you du for 'er?"

George: "I give 'er a bottle o' turpentine."

They met again a month later at Acle.

Said Amos: "George, boy, do you mind telling me last time we met that you drenched your mare for colic with turpentine?"

George: "Oh, ah."

Amos: "I drenched mine with turpentine and she died."

George: "So did mine."

Sir Hubert Newton, Hon. M.A. (Keele),
Chairman, Britannia Building Society.

I think one of the comments reserved for the Speaker's Grace is worthwhile quoting:

"Lord, fill my mouth with worthwhile stuff and nudge me when I've said enough."

Sir David Nicolson,
Formerly Chairman, British Airways.

There are three sorts of people in this world; those who make things happen, those who watch things happening, and those who don't know what is happening. Let us try to be members of the first group if we possibly can.

Germany's famous 'Iron Chancellor' Bismarck was reputed to have said that there were four basic qualities in man: energy, idleness, stupidity and intelligence. The man who was both idle and stupid could be made use of by application of the boot. The man who was energetic and intelligent was most useful and suitable for positions like Chief of Staff. The man who was idle and intelligent was suited for high command. But the man who was energetic and stupid was a menace and should be removed forthwith.

Professor Stanley D. Nisbet,
Professor of Education, University of Glasgow, 1951-78.

One winter's evening in 1941, I was one of 24 airmen due to go on guard duty at an R.A.F. station. The normal drill was as follows. Each man on the list had to go to the armoury at 18.00, collect a rifle and ammunition, parade for instructions, and then spend the night walking around the camp looking for enemy parachutists — a wearisome and unpopular duty.

On this particular evening I got to know that there were at the moment only 12 rifles in the armoury. I quickly advised my friends to hang back till the available rifles had been collected. (We could never be made to go on guard duty without rifles, could we?)

So we waited till 12 innocents had collected their arms and then we feigned surprise when we were told there were no more. But still had to parade. The 12 with rifles stood at one side and the 12 without at the other.

The Flight-Sergeant who came to 'take the parade' was an irascible old-stager, experienced in guard-duty procedure but new to this particular station and its arrangements. He roared out:

"Old and new guards, atten——tion!"

We all jumped to attention, a bit puzzled. The awful truth began to dawn on us when the next bellow came:

"Old guard — prepare to hand over your arms to new guard!"

No one dared say a word. The transfer of arms duly took place, the 'old guard' barely concealing their sadistic glee. We knew what was coming next — and it came:

"Old guard — dis——miss!"

The background music for our subsequent instructions was the distant sound of uncontrolled laughter. How can one's fellow men be so unkind?

HALT!
WHO DOESN'T
GO THERE?

204

Colonel Geoffrey W. Noakes, O.B.E., T.D., D.L., J.P.,
Formerly Managing Director, William Timpson Ltd.

A very eminent gentleman rang up and asked my daughter Elizabeth if I could be persuaded to make a speech at a dinner he was chairing. The answer he got was:

"Your Grace, you would have very much more difficulty in persuading him not to."

The Rev. Dr. Edward R. Norman,
Dean of Peterhouse, Cambridge.

At a recent gathering of churchmen in the United States, I found myself in conversation with three others, who were plainly taking exception to what I was saying. Each time I spoke of the Christian view of man they all chorused "and *woman*".

Finally, after I had referred to the Almighty as 'Him' I was explicitly ticked off, in shocked moralistic tones, for using sexist language. Not wishing to be difficult, and anxious to observe the customs of the society, I endeavoured to make amends and generally to brighten up the moment with a silly joke about the round towers of Ireland — those tall, thin structures, like Celtic factory chimneys, which are a glory of that country's religious heritage — viz: that St. Patrick had instructed the monks to dig wells, but that they had held the plans upside-down. It was not the right thing to have said. Desperately seeking some clue as to the nature of my further solecism, I then noticed the names upon the identification badges my colleagues had stuck in their lapels.

They were called O'Connell, O'Donnell and Murphy.

Admiral Sir William O'Brien, K.C.B., D.S.C.,
Rear-Admiral of the United Kingdom.

In 1940, just prior to the fall of France, the Naval Expeditionary Force abandoned its task of mining the Rhine and made its way westwards. In a village called Sézanne the officers were billeted for a while in an orphanage, whose distraught proprietors were deeply concerned for the future of their charges. I grew very fond of a little boy called Andrée. This friendship was observed by authority and the child briefed accordingly.

Next morning, as I was leaving the building, Andrée ran up to me calling out:

"Bonjour, papa! Bonjour, papa!"

A large bearded sailor standing nearby, looked up, smiled and said:

"Hello, sir, been here before?"

The deck of an aircraft carrier was a very dark place in which to work during night flying. The leading aircraft handler was trying to collect his tractor team together during a lull between sorties. Aircraft Handler Brown, of West Indian extraction, was missing.

"Brown, where are you?" yelled the leading hand.

"Here, Leading Hand, here," replied Brown.

"Can't see you, where the hell are you?"

"Just here, Leading Hand."

"Well, smile, you bastard, so I can tell where you are."

Major-General William Odling, C.B., O.B.E., M.C., D.L.,
Chief of Staff, Far East Land Forces, until 1964.

Johnny (to his mother): "I don't want to go to school today."

Mother: "Why not? You haven't been for five days."

Johnny: "The girls tease me, the boys bully me, the staff are unsympathetic."

Mother: "Pull your socks up, Johnny. You're 49 now and the headmaster."

Professor Robert M. Ogilvie, F.B.A., F.R.S.E., F.S.A., F.S.A.Scot.,
Professor of Humanity, University of St. Andrews.

My grandfather, Professor A.B. Macaulay, knew a great theologian. He was, as I remember him, almost a teetotaller, except for whisky. He used to relax on Mondays by playing a round of golf on the links, and might carry a small flask with him. One icy January he slipped and fell. As he got up he felt a drip down his trouser-leg.

"Losh," he said, "I hope it's blood!"

A primary school class near my home was asked to draw a picture of 'The Flight into Egypt'. There were various versions, one ingenious — a Boeing 707 with Mary, Joseph and Jesus and someone else.

"Who is that?" asked the teacher.

"Oh," said the child, "that's Pontius the Pilot."

The Hon. Angus Ogilvy,
President, Imperial Cancer Research Fund.

I remember Selwyn Lloyd telling me a long time ago that he went to a dinner at which the famous Lord Birkenhead was present. During the course of the dinner there was a lull in the conversation, and somebody asked Lord Birkenhead what were the three great milestones in his life. Lord Birkenhead remained silent for a few moments, then said:

"The first when I heard that I'd got a double first at Oxford. I suppose the second was when I was made a K.C., and the third was when I became Lord Chancellor."

His wife, who was sitting next to Selwyn, chipped in and said:

"But darling, what about the day we got married?" To which Lord Birkenhead replied, without a moment's hesitation:

"My dear, I think you must be getting a little deaf. We are talking about milestones — not millstones."

Professor Richard A.C. Oliver,
Emeritus Professor of Education at the University of Manchester.

Colleges of education were formerly not renowned for the calibre of their students. A university professor was invited to give a course of lectures at one of the men's colleges. He was afterwards asked whether he had noticed any difference between his university audiences and his college audiences. He thought for a moment, then replied:

"Come to think of it, I have. When I go into a university lecture I say, 'Good morning, gentlemen', and they reply, 'Good morning, sir'. When I go into a college lecture I say, 'Good morning, gentlemen', and they write it down."

Parental hopes and expectations are not always easy to live up to. An undergraduate had been having a good time at his university, but unfortunately failed his finals. He wired to his sister at home:

"FAILED FINALS STOP PREPARE FATHER."

He received the reply: "FATHER PREPARED STOP PREPARE YOURSELF."

The Late Lieut.-General Sir William Oliver, G.B.E., K.C.B., K.C.M.G., D.L.,
British High Commissioner in Australia, 1959–65.

When Sir Robert Menzies was Prime Minister of Australia he travelled extensively during the winter recess, usually to England, where he combined the business of political discussions with the pleasure of watching cricket; and to the U.S.A. where he would see the President.

On his return he would normally address the House of Representatives on world affairs, early in the spring session, to give an account of his stewardship, as it were: on these occasions the Diplomatic Corps would attend in force to hear what he had to say. I was present on one particular evening and, as the Prime Minister entered the house and approached the Dispatch Box, an exuberant member of the Opposition, who seemed to have come straight from the dining room, called out, amidst laughter:

"It's good to see you back, Bob, you seem to spend half your ruddy time overseas."

Sir Robert turned towards the speaker and bowed slightly.

"I thank you, sir," he said, "and I am sure that the Right Honourable Member will agree with me that it is better to spend half one's time overseas than all one's time half seas over."

Even the Opposition joined in the laughter.

Professor Patrick G. O'Neill,
Professor of Japanese, University of London.

A film-producer friend went out for dinner with some business colleagues to an exclusive London restaurant which prided itself on its haute cuisine. When it came to his turn to order, he said that he would like fish fingers.

"Yes, sir, " said the waiter, without the slightest change of expression, "— Birds Eye or Findus?"

William George Onslow, C.B.,
Formerly Chairman, Yorkshire and Humberside Economic Planning Board.

I am a very poor golfer and had never won anything in my life. But on this particular day everything went right and I won the Challenge Cup. I stayed on after the presentation for a few beers and arrived home rather late. I walked in holding the trophy above my head and showing it to my wife. To my surprise there was silence until she said:

"I can see that you've had a good day, but it's very late; come and have your dinner and stop the fooling."

"But I've won it, at golf, on a golf course; other people were playing."

"Yes, I'm sure you did very well, but it's very late. You've had your little joke. It's too late tonight, you can take it back in the morning."

Sir Duncan Oppenheim,
Formerly Chairman, British-American Tobacco Co. Ltd.

At wedding receptions one is accustomed to laughing politely at stale, feeble jokes retailed in the speeches. It was a pleasure, therefore, some years ago to listen to a charming, witty and appropriate speech made by the clergyman, uncle of the bride, at the end of which speech he said:

"I suppose, being a clergyman, I am expected to conclude by giving some moral guidance to the young couple. I would, therefore, remind them that marriage is for once only — for life, that is what is called monotony — sorry, I mean monogamy."

Lord Oram,
A Lord in Waiting (Government Whip), 1976–78.

One morning my wife received from my tax collector a letter which began thus:

"Dear Lady Oram, I was sorry to hear of the death of your husband but we must settle certain tax matters concerning his estate..."

I had been staying in London the night before so on receiving the letter my wife phoned me just in case the tax man had heard something of which she was not aware. Her voice betrayed neither anxiety, nor indeed relief when she heard my voice.

What had happened was as follows:

I had been receiving for two years a pension in respect of some twenty years' service in the House of Commons. I then became a Peer and a Front Bench spokesman in the Lords on trade, industry and other subjects. Technically I was a Lord-in-Waiting, a ministerial post carrying a modest salary which disqualified me from receiving the House of Commons pension and I had so notified the authorities. Apparently when the tax official received news that my pension had stopped he could think of only one reason for it and wrote accordingly to my wife.

Of course, I then drafted a letter to him. I did so with some care since he might have wondered where it had come from. Among other things I asked if he had consulted my doctor whom I had not seen for some time. Also I assured him that although I had become a Lord-in-Waiting to Her Majesty it was considered to be a post of some honour and was not as deadly as he might think.

I was glad to get from him an impeccable reply. He apologised "for having assumed my demise" which was much nicer than merely saying he thought I was dead.

Professor Robin Orr, C.B.E.,
Composer; Professor of Music, Cambridge University, and Fellow of
St. John's College, 1965–76.

For some years I used to travel frequently on the early morning train from Cambridge to Edinburgh. Luncheon was served between Newcastle upon Tyne and Berwick upon Tweed; and in those days it was a rough ride. I soon settled for tomato juice rather than soup, which invariably slopped all over the table. One day when the going became alarmingly rough I said to the guard who happened to be passing;

"Can't you ask him to drive a bit slower?"

"No, sir," he replied, "if he doesna' make up time he'll no' get his bonus."

About a week later there was a serious derailment in this sector. As we passed slowly by the scene the following day I overheard the restaurant steward say to the guard:

"And where's the derailment to be today?" The reply was moderately comforting: "It's already happened at Waverley but it was only a wee one."

There was once a Fellow of my College who developed a liking for a bottle or two of burgundy before breakfast. This habit was evidently frowned upon in his home so he had to resort to some other place and the empty bottles would later be found standing by the wash-basins in the Fellows' cloakroom. The Junior Bursar, or some interfering busybody, suggested to him that he might surely be able to find a more appropriate place to dispose of them. Some days later a distinguished guest was being helped into one of the visitors' gowns before going in to dine. A heavy clunking noise led to the embarrassing discovery of an empty bottle in the bag-like foot of each sleeve.

But for what else, one may ask, were those long sleeves intended? In these days when husbands share the domestic chores I am surprised I have never yet seen a don shopping in his gown; ideal for a French loaf and a salmon.

Major-General John I.H. Owen, O.B.E.,
Chef de Cabinet to Chartered Accountants.

I like the story of the Irishman who couldn't understand why his sister had three brothers and he had only two!

Many years ago, a marine appeared at one of my 'orderly rooms' on a charge of drunkenness. As it was his seventeenth offence, he was duly punished and I delivered a homily on drinking, etc., and ended by saying that I would like to see him again in six months to see whether he had taken note of my advice.

Six months later I saw a cheerful bright marine who thanked me for my advice; he'd given up drink and, with the money he had saved thereby, he would now be requesting to buy himself his discharge from the corps.

Rear-Admiral Ronald W. Paffard, C.B., C.B.E. (Retired).

While serving in the Admiralty nearly thirty years ago I sat on a committee which met once a week to streamline the complex scale of naval allowances. Our deliberations entailed very frequent reference to the King's Regulations and Admiralty Instructions, a large volume commonly referred to for short as 'K.R.'

At our first meeting in the present reign the chairman reminded us that we were now governed by the *Queen's* Regulations and would we please try to remember to refer to 'Q.R.', not 'K.R.'

We usually remembered, but there were occasional lapses which were invariably corrected loudly by one member, a civil servant who otherwise took almost no part in our discussions and was on the committee for no very obvious reason. We got rather fed up with his officious interruptions. Towards the end of the meeting the chairman said:

"Well, gentlemen, I think that's all we can deal with today. Next week we'll have to tackle the tricky business of K.U.A."

"Mr. Chairman, please — Q.U.A.," protested the officious member. There was a moment's stunned silence and then a roar of laughter. He was the only one present who did not know the customary abbreviation for Kit Upkeep Allowance.

Ernest John Pakes, C.B.E.,
Formerly President of the Associated Chambers of Commerce of India.

I am now 81 years of age, so here's a suitable story:
> Old age is golden, I've heard it said;
> But sometimes I wonder, as I get into bed,
> With my ears in a drawer, my teeth in a cup,
> My eyes on the table until I wake up.
> Ere sleep dims my eyes, I say to myself,
> "Is there anything else I should lay on the shelf?"

Admiral Sir Frederick Parham, G.B.E., K.C.B., D.S.O.,
Commander-in-Chief, The Nore, 1955–58.

The captain of one of the British cruisers, covering a Russian convoy in the Arctic, who fought and shadowed *Scharnhorst* for about ten hours on

26th December, 1943, until she was sunk by a force led by *Duke of York*, eventually clambered onto his bunk, very cold and tired, for a brief sleep. A few hours later he was called by his young steward with a cup of tea. The captain opened his eyes and said:

"That was rather a good little show yesterday, wasn't it?" To which the young steward replied:

"Well, sir, it makes a change!"

Two young Royal Marine Commando officers were in their London club boasting about "the splendid men whom they had the honour to command — brave, tough in adversity, etc., etc.". At last an apoplectic retired Army officer, sitting near them, could stand it no longer.

"You young fellows," he said, "don't know what you are talking about: your men are nothing like the men I commanded. I remember, in the Ashanti war I came across one of my men — poor fellah — pinned to a tree by an assegai. I said to him: 'Good gad, man, are you in pain?' And he said: 'Well, sir, it hurts when I laugh!'."

A famous — and dearly loved — Admiral of the Fleet once told my wife and myself that he considered that it was essential that he should enlarge his house — and in particular build an extra bathroom — "with all these grandchildren about".

"Ah, yes," said my wife, "I know — too many celluloid ducks."

"Celluloid ducks, my foot," said the admiral, "wait till *you* have got into the bath and sat on a soldier with fixed bayonet!"

Signals exchanged after a destroyer collided with the admiral's cruiser flagship:

Flag officer to captain of destroyer:

"What do you propose to do now?"

Reply: "Buy a farm."

**Vice-Admiral Sir John Parker, K.B.E., C.B., D.S.C.,
Former Assistant, Chief of Defence Staff, 1963–66.**

Joe Kelly (Admiral Sir John Kelly, C.-in-C. Portsmouth) is reputed to have said to a sailor, at a time when, through mobilisation of large numbers, saluting between officers and men was not all that it might be:

"His Majesty King George has ordered that you and I should salute each other: you start!"

**Sir Peter Parker, M.V.O.,
Chairman, British Rail Board.**

This is a true story.

I had just left Oxford and was doing a research fellowship at Cornell in 1950. My subject, which was to do with research in what makes people work, or want to work, was abbreviated and given a new title for my American tour. I found on notice boards what I was doing was called 'The Dynamics of Labour'. And in those days 'dynamics' was an unusual word; I felt inches taller if a little bemused.

About five or six months later a girl friend who was a doctor, and whom I had known well at Oxford, rang up from New York. She explained on the phone to me at Cornell, in Upper New York State, that she also had a research fellowship and when I asked about it, she said she was examining the consumption of oxygen during childbirth. She explained about balancing some machine on mums' tums, and when I reacted in a baffled way she said it was perfectly all right because they had simplified the whole thing for her. She said they called it 'The Dynamics of Labour'. I knew then we were meant for each other. And we married and have been happy ever after.

**Sir William Parker, Bt.,
Retired Railway Officer.**

This story concerns a tribe of pygmies.

One poor little fellow developed nasty sores around his thighs. He went to the witch doctor for help, and was given various remedies, both herbal and magical. But all to no purpose — the sores got steadily worse.

The poor wee man's faith in the witch doctor's ability gradually waned, and he decided to risk his jealousy and wrath and visit the white doctor who he knew lived at the big settlement 120 miles down the river. It was a long and dangerous journey but, after some months, he returned, cured. The witch doctor was indeed furious, if a trifle impressed.

"What could the white doctor do for you that I couldn't do for you?"

"He cut nine inches off the tops of my wellington boots!"

This is the story of the railway officer who didn't get promoted.

The career he had chosen was not one in which a man gets rich quickly — or indeed, ever at all; but he had shown considerable aptitude, and quickly rose from the ranks to the junior grade of management. But there he stuck. It was in the operating department (as it was then called), and his friends and colleagues were at first puzzled that such a bright fellow never even got short-listed for interviews when he applied for a job. But, gradually, he became accepted as a piece of the office furniture, and it was not until his retirement nearly 30 years later that one of them plucked up courage to ask him the reason why. And he replied:

"Well, it's rather a sore point, really. When I got this position as Assistant to the District Operating Superintendent, all went well until I got married, and my wife got increasingly impatient and frustrated when I was 'on call' and every five or six nights the phone rang and Control told me that a wagon had come off the road at so and so, generally a branch line which was well and truly blocked. Off I had to go to the Control office, to appraise myself of the position and then on to the site of the accident, probably in a freezing fog on a February morning, around two o'clock.

"So we devised a plan. We bought a good-looking young ape, and, after months of patient training, we taught him to dress in my clothes whenever the phone rang at night; then to drive the car, and finally to go to the Control office. This worked like a charm, and we enjoyed blissful, peaceful nights...

"Until one night, something happened which, it turned out later, affected a main line, and was serious enough for the District Superintendent to turn out in person. And the chap we had then was damned clever. He was also very observant, and immediately recognised that the ape wasn't me...and that, Charles, is why I remained an 'Assistant to'.

"What does still gall me, though, is that the ape is now a District Manager!"

Professor Robin Pedley,
Yorkshire Dalesman and Author.

Here are two stories from Swaledale:

A local resident was a great champion of the rights of villagers against the local aristocracy, particularly concerning common land and rights of way. One day, as he was walking over Grinton Moor, he was accosted by the angry master of the Great Hall:

"What are you doing here, my man? You're disturbing the grouse! Get off my land!"

"Oh, aye?" (slowly). "An' what mak's t' think it's *thy* land?"

Master (bursting with rage): "How dare you speak to me like that! This land's been in my family for hundreds of years. My ancestors fought for it!"

"Aye? Then tak' thi coat off, and Ah'll fight thee for 't!"

Two visitors came to Swaledale on a walking holiday. They booked in at Grinton's village inn, and set out one morning to walk up and over the moors to the even smaller village of Keld at the head of the dale.

The early sun shone brightly as they swung along moorland tracks and green roads, and at midday they sat down contentedly to eat their lunch. A shepherd passed by with his flock and they asked, more by way of conversation than anything else:

"How far is it to Keld?"

"Keld? Oh, it must be about seven mile."

A bit further away than they'd expected; so on they went under the now hot sun — down into the ghylls, clambering up and out again, through the thick heather and bracken; on and on. In the late afternoon they passed a lone farmhouse, where the wife was feeding her hens.

"Can you tell us how far it is to Keld?"

"Keld? Well, I think it's about seven mile."

Dismay. But nothing for it but to go on; climbing the peaks, running out of paths and even sheep-trods, across the endless heather, while the sun sank remorselessly into the west.

At last they dropped down into the valley, where a narrow packhorse bridge crossed the river. Leaning over it in contemplation of the waters below was an old man. Trudging up to him they put the all-important question. The old man took off his cap and scratched his head, deliberating his response. Then:

"Keld?" he said, still ruminatively. "Why, I'd say it's just about seven mile."

And one visitor turned to the other and said:

"Thank God! We're holding our own!"

Vice-Admiral Sir Arthur Pedder, K.B.E. C.B.,
Formerly Commander, Allied Naval Forces, Northern Europe.

In the spring of 1956 when I was commanding the British aircraft carriers, I was sent out to China with two carriers and told by Admiral Mountbatten, then First Sea Lord, to stop off in Bombay and persuade Mr. Nehru and his Cabinet that India should obtain a second-hand carrier from us.

So it was arranged that Mr. Nehru and half his Cabinet and Mr. Morarji Desai, who was then the Governor of Bombay, should join my Flagship at sea off Bombay by means of an R.I.N. destroyer. And so they did, and so too came Mr. Nehru's little daughter, Indira.

We laid on a 'Carrier Spectacular', which can be quite impressive, and then set course for Bombay. I then received a signal, 'Personal, Operational, Immediate', from the First Sea Lord, saying that because of street rioting in Bombay I was to fly them by helicopter to the airfield. So preparations were made.

Very soon after, I received another signal of the same priority from the Fifth Sea Lord, who was in charge of Naval Aviation, and a friend of mine. It said, in so many words: "The power-operated controls of your helicopters may suddenly fail, in which case they can only be put down immediately on to whatever is below them." Just for fun, I sent my friend a signal of the same urgency and priority thus: "Your signal timed so and so, please see First Sea Lord's signal timed so and so. What does A do?" Back came the expected reply: "Any action you take will be entirely your own responsibility."

So up to the flight deck went Nehru and Morarji Desai, Indira Gandhi and me. I started to put Mr. Nehru into a 'Mae West' and show him how to operate it. He said: "Why do I need this? Aren't your helicopters safe?" I laughed and assured him that they were, and he laughed too, and the cameras clicked. I have the picture in my album.

It is now of great interest to me that while Mr. Nehru talked almost continuously while he was on board, Indira just listened and never said a word. I thought that she might have ambitions!

Michael Pertwee,
Playwright and Screenwriter.

There was this old Indian chief on a reservation, who was reputed to have a quite incredible memory for anything that had ever happened to him or been said to him. I was taken to see him as quite a young man and the friend who took me asked the old chief what he had had for breakfast exactly twenty-four years earlier to the day. After a brief pause the old man said:

"Four eggs."

Fifteen years later by chance, I happened to be back at the same spot and, to my amazement, I saw the old chief still sitting in his same place. I hurried up to him and in traditional fashion said:

"How!"

To which, without hesitation, he replied:

"Fried."

Professor Owen Hood Phillips, Q.C., J.P., D.C.L.,
Emeritus Professor of Jurisprudence at the University of Birmingham.

A young curate, newly ordained, was advised by his vicar to study carefully a collection of sermons by the former Bishop of London, Dr. Winnington-Ingram. The curate took this advice, and began his first sermon with the words:

"When I was Bishop of Stepney..."

It is still the custom for members of the Bar to wear hats, usually bowlers. One of the judges, on leaving a hotel after a well-attended legal function, was gratified that the cloakroom attendant handed him his hat without asking to see the ticket.

"How did you know this was my hat?" asked the judge.

"I didn't," replied the cloakroom attendant, "but it's the one you gave me."

Among many stories told about Serjeant Sullivan, the last Serjeant of the Irish Bar to practise in the English courts, the following is typical.

A case that originated in the west of Ireland finally found its way to the House of Lords on appeal. One of their Lordships evidently did not think much of Serjeant Sullivan's legal argument, for he interrupted him by asking:

"I presume, Serjeant Sullivan, that your clients are familiar with the maxim: *Assignatus utitur jure auctoris?*"

The learned Serjeant promptly replied:

"Indeed, my Lord; back home in Ballynattery they talk of nothing else."

Surgeon Rear Admiral Arnold Pomfret, C.B., O.B.E. (Retired).

The doctor's telephone rang at two a.m. An excited man's voice said:

"Please come quickly, I'm sure my wife has appendicitis." The doctor took particulars and, suddenly remembering, said:

"But I removed your wife's appendix two years ago and you know as well as I do she hasn't got another."

"I know that," said the man, "but *I've* got another wife."

An old destroyer acquired a new commanding officer. The ship's company was fallen-in and the old captain made his farewell speech, introduced his successor, and left.

The new C.O. looked the crew over and said:

"Before anything else, let me stress this isn't my ship, it isn't your ship, it's our ship."

A voice muttered: "Good! Let's sell it."

Sir Hilton Poynton, G.C.M.G., Formerly Permanent Under-Secretary of State, Colonial Office.

Nowadays the term 'credibility' (or lack of) is frequently on the lips of critics of our political leaders and others. I am reminded of an occasion when one of my aunts took her two young children to Madame Tussaud's. (As both children are now in their seventies, it will be appreciated that this was many years ago.) Like many another before and since, my aunt was taken in by the waxwork policeman standing just inside the door, and asked him a question. Then, realising her mistake, she said apologetically:

"I am so sorry. Do you know, for a moment I quite thought you were real."

The Rt. Hon. Reg Prentice, M.P., Minister for Social Security; Ex-Minister for Overseas Development.

A Minister of the Crown was addressing a village meeting in the West Country in support of Government policies.

"We will cut down Government spending," he explained, "and this will help us to fight inflation."

Voice at back: "Ah! but when be all this going to 'appen?"

Ignoring the heckler, the minister went on: "We will cut down on the bureaucracy and make things more efficient."

Voice at back: "Ah! but when be all this going to 'appen?"

He decided he must deal with the heckler, so he asked:

"Do you work on a farm?"

"Ah!"

"Well, suppose you put a prize bull into a field of cows, you would expect good results, but you would not expect to see those results the next morning, would you?"

There was a pause, then came the retort:

"No, but next morning I'd expect to see more contented faces around than I can see 'ere."

Lieut.-General Sir Steuart Pringle, Bt., Commandant General, Royal Marines.

Consternation reigned in the offices of Amalgamated Aerospace when two of the three prototypes of their new airliner crashed on their initial flights.

"The cause," said the chairman, "is clearly a design fault. In both cases the wings have torn off at the roots. Rebuilding with stronger spars would add £10 million to the unit cost. Do you have a better idea?" He glowered at the serried ranks of the design team.

Silence — until the newest-joined member of the team suggested cutting a row of slots along the root of each wing. He advanced no theory for his idea, but the computer supported it, and commercial pressure is commercial pressure.

The third prototype flew like a bird. Many glasses of champagne later, the design genius revealed his secret.

"In my last job, I worked for a firm of toilet paper manufacturers. We never could get it to tear at the perforations."

Although the wine produced by a certain Mediterranean island was not noted for its quality, one firm had been particularly successful. Now the founder of the business was dying and his three sons gathered round the old man's bedside to hear his dying words hoping, in particular, to learn the secret part of the winemaking process he had always kept to himself. Life was fading fast.

"My boys," he gasped, "the secret is…" they leaned forward as strength ebbed with every gasp, "…you can also make it with grapes."

The Hon. Terence Prittie, M.B.E.,
Author and Journalist; Escaped six times when P.o.W. in Germany.

A friend suffered from his wife's belief that he had real 'taste'. So when he arrived home from work she had a maddening habit of asking him to come shopping with her ("Just time, darling") and look at dresses, chinaware, umbrellas and the rest.

One evening he arrived back from the office, very tired. Sure enough:

"Something I *do* want you to help me choose, darling."

So off they went. She was after underwear — expensive underwear, he noted wearily, as she examined the goods. Then:

"I think this is just *me*, don't you, darling?" She held up the satin panties as shop assistants stood dutifully around; and suddenly inspiration came to him:

"They look lovely, but what would your *husband* say?"

He lived happily ever after, able to come home, pour himself a drink, put his feet up, relax.

General Charles de Gaulle was taken to an exhibition of French impressionist paintings. He stopped and stared:

"Tiens, un Monet?"

"No, mon Général, it is a Manet."

They moved on: "Well, this one is — a Gauguin!"

"Mon Général, it is a painting of 'le Douanier' Rousseau."

De Gaulle tried once more: "Ah, but *this* is a veritable Picasso!"

"Alas, mon Général, it is a mirror."

Harry Rabinowitz, M.B.E.,
Musical Director, Conductor and Composer; Formerly Head of Music,
London Weekend Television.

The concert had been near-disastrous, but the mayoral reception looked like being worse. The woodwind had whined, the strings had screeched and the brass had brayed. In the concerto, try as he might, the eminent maestro had not been able to coax the City Orchestra to play at the same tempo as the soloist; at one point he had hissed at the latter:

"Don't look now, but I think we're being followed!" And now he was faced by the boring mayor, fluting about culture and beneficence and enthusing about the performance.

Eventually, the question had to come:

"And when was the last time you conducted our orchestra?"

The maestro drew himself up to his full height: "Tonight."

Sir Ralph Richardson,
Actor.

The play was well into the second act, the actors were burbling along, there was not much response from the audience; it did not seem to be required. Suddenly from the stalls a man stood up and said (not very loudly, but clearly):

"IS THERE A DOCTOR IN THE HOUSE?" There was a tremor in the audience. The actors were not disturbed and continued, but the man remained standing. After a few moments, from the dress circle, a shy little form half rose: "Ah, yes," he said, "I — I am a doctor."

The man in the stalls turned to him:

"Oh, doctor," he called, "isn't this a TERRIBLE PLAY?"

Arnold Ridley,
Author, Playwright, Actor and Producer.

For some unknown reason I have an acute dislike of the term 'Show Business' but must confess that since I made my first professional stage engagement in the autumn of 1913, I seem to have been connected with almost every form of entertainment and in nearly every capacity. Amongst these is the BBC sound serial 'The Archers', in which I appeared *ad hoc* as Doughy Hood, the village baker.

Members of 'The Archers' were often offered social engagements and, amongst these, I was invited to travel as Doughy Hood to Swansea and there to declare open a large multiple bakery to be started in the borough. This I did, to the best of my ability, but was rather surprised shortly afterwards to find myself assailed by a very angry Welshwoman who addressed me in furiously angry terms:

"How dare you come down here pretending you're Doughy Hood!" she shouted. "They should have the law on you." I was so surprised that I couldn't think of anything to say.

"You're nothing but an imposter," she continued — "that's the word — imposter!"

She paused for breath before proceeding in a milder tone:

"Mind you," she said, "You *sound* like him. Yes, I grant you that — you sound *like* him, but he's a tall thin man, not a bit like you!"

It's certainly a proof of the mental appearance created by the listener dependent upon the artist's only asset — his voice — since I'm only five foot nine inches and grown robust in build.

**The Hon. Nicholas Ridley, M.P.,
Minister of State, Foreign and Commonwealth Office.**

An event in Parliament during the Labour administration in 1977 comes to my mind.

The Conservatives moved a vote of no confidence in the Labour Government. The Liberal party supported the Government, thus saving it. It was at this point I felt moved to say:

"I have heard of rats leaving a sinking ship, but I have never heard of mice joining one."

Over six hundred contributors sent stories to OXFAM for this book; unfortunately, through lack of space, we have not been able to include all of them. In addition, several stories were received from different sources: in this case, the published version is the one received first.

The publishers and directors of OXFAM gratefully acknowledge all these contributions below.

Lord Abinger, DL
Brigadier Peter B.E. Acland, OBE, MC, TD
General Sir Ronald F. Adam, Bt, GCB, DSO, OBE
Sir Campbell Adamson
Lord Airedale
Sir Donald Allen, OBE, MC
Major-General Robert H. Allen, CB
Dame Peggy Ashcroft, DBE
Lord Avebury
Lord Aylestone, PC, CH, CBE

Lord Baker, OBE, FRS
Major-General Peter Baldwin
Sir Joseph Balmer, JP
Professor Michael Banton, JP
The Rt. Rev. Cuthbert Bardsley, CBE, DD
Sir Henry Barnard
Major-General Richard H. Barry, CB, CBE
Sir Cecil Bateman, KBE
Edgar C. Bate-Smith, CBE
Sir Darrell Bates, CMG, CVO
Peter C. Bayley
Wing-Commander E. Bentley Beauman
Lord Beaumont of Whitley
David Beavis, CBE

Professor Arnold E. Bender
Professor Maurice W. Beresford
John Berry, CBE, FRSE, DL
Derek J. Bibby, MC
John C. Bidgood
Air Vice-Marshal Harold A.C. Bird-Wilson, CBE, DSO, DFC, AFC
Lord Birkett
Ian Hervey Stuart Black
Captain Ronald W. Blacklock, CBE, DSC
Sir Francis Blake, Bt
Major-General Adam J.C. Block, CB, CBE, DSO
Professor John W. Boag
Professor Walter F. Bodmer, FRS
The Hon. Major-General Eric L. Bols, CB, DSO
Major-General Henry M.G. Bond, JP, DL
Professor Sir Hermann Bondi, KCB, FRS
Robert E. Boote, CVO
Judge James Booth
Major-General Alexander C.S. Boswell, CBE
Sir Anthony Bowlby, Bt
Sir Bernard Braine, DL, MP
Colonel Hugh T. Brassey, OBE, MC
Judge Sir Peter Bristow

Major-General Robert W.T. Britten, CB, MC

Professor Robert J. Brocklehurst, DM

Major-General Robert S. Broke, CB, OBE, MC

Major-General William M. Broomhall, CB, DSO, OBE

Montague Calman, FRSA

Wyn Calvin

Field Marshal Sir James Cassels, GCB, KBE, DSO

Lance Cattermole, ROI

Air Marshal Sir Edward Chilton, KBE, CB

Captain Arthur W. Clarke, CBE, DSO

Major-General P.F. Claxton, CB, OBE

Brian G.H. Clegg

Lord Clifford of Chudleigh, OBE, DL

Professor John L. Cloudsley-Thompson

Major-General Ronald Coaker, CB, CBE, MC

Commander Kenneth Cohen, CB, CMG

Rear-Admiral George K. Collett, CB, DSC

Sir John Colville, CB, CVO

Sir John Compton Miller, MBE, TD

Professor John T. Coppock, FBA, FRSE

Colonel John L. Corbett-Winder, OBE, MC, JP

Sir Kenneth Corley

Professor Ronald J. Cornish

Sir John Cotterell, Bt

Sir Alan Cottrell, FRS

Captain John S. Crawford, DSO, OBE, RN

Lieut.-Colonel Richard Crawshaw, OBE, TD, DL, MP

Lord Croham, GCB

Professor Henry A. Cronne

Professor Bernard Crossland, CBE

Sir Samuel Curran, FRS

Tam Dalyell, MP

Major-General Roy B. Darkin, CBE

Lord Darwen

The Rt. Hon. Sir Geoffrey de Freitas, KCMG

Sir Richard Denby

Lord Denham

Sir Eric de Normann, KBE, CB

Professor Duncan Derrett

Dermot H. de Trafford, VRD

Brigadier Michael P.D. Dewar, CB, CBE

Major-General Richard H. Dewing, CB, DSO, MC

Professor Thorold Dickinson, CBE

Professor Charles H. Dobinson, CMG

The Rt. Hon. Sir John Donaldson

The Bishop of Dorking

Sir Sholto Douglas, Bt, MC

Air Vice-Marshal John Downey, CB, DFC, AFC

Graham R. Dowson

Judge John F. Drabble

Sir Arthur Drew, KCB, JP
Lord Dulverton, CBE, TD, DL
Sir Kingsley Dunham, FRS
Alastair M. Dunnett
Sir Simon Dunning, Bt

Sir Hugh Elliott, Bt, OBE
Major-General James G. Elliott, CIE
Sir Norman Elliott, CBE
Air Marshal Sir Thomas Elmhirst, KBE, CB, AFC
Lord Elton, TD
Sir Charles Empson, KCMG
Sir Basil Engholm, KCB
Major-General Edward Estcourt, DSO, OBE
Lord Evans of Claughton
The Late Major-General Sir Robert Ewbank, KBE, CB, DSO
The Late Professor Sir Alexander Ewing
Thomas Erle Faber
Sir James Falconer, MBE, JP
Professor Edward D. Farmer
Sir Eric Faulkner, MBE
Ian H.F. Findlay
Professor D. J. Finney, CBE, FRS
Sir John Fletcher-Cooke, CMG
The Late Lieut.-General Arthur N. Floyer-Acland, CB, DSO, MC, DL
Colonel Sir John Forbes, Bt, DSO, DL, JP
Professor William G.G. Forrest
Sir Stafford Foster-Sutton, KBE, CMG, QC
Professor Alastair D.S. Fowler, FBA
Sir Eric Franklin, CBE

Major-General Richard G.F. Frisby, CB, CBE, DSO, MC
Air Vice-Marshal E. L. Frith, CB
Sir John Fry, Bt
Sir Stephen Furness, Bt

Professor William A. Gambling
Sir Ronald Garvey, KCMG, KCVO, MBE
Major David Gibson
Lord Gibson-Watt, MC, DL
Sir Derek Gilbey, Bt
Sir Angus Gillan, KBE, CMG
Colonel Sir John E. Gilmour, Bt, DSO, TD, DL, JP
The Bishop of Gloucester
Lieut.-Colonel William Gordon, CBE, MC
Major-General Robert Gordon-Finlayson, OBE, JP, DL
Lord Gorell
Sir William Gorell Barnes, KCMG, CB
Professor A.D.M. Greenfield, CBE
Major-General Sir Stuart Greeves, KBE, CB, DSO, MC
Major-General Guy P. Gregson, CB, CBE, DSO, MC
Sir Harold Grime, JP, DL
The Late Sir Kenneth Grubb, KCMG

Earl Haig, OBE
Lord Hale
Major-General M.C.K. Halford, DSO, OBE, DL
Professor Peter Hall

Sir Charles Hallinan, CBE, KCSG, OStJ

Sir Lincoln Hallinan, DL

Sir Richard Hamilton, Bt

Air Chief Marshal Sir Donald I. Hardman, GBE, KCB, DFC

Sir James Harford, KBE, CMG

Robert Harris

Major-General Eric Harrison, CB, CBE, MC

Sidney Harrison

Professor R.J. Harrison-Church

Sir William Hayter, KCMG

Bertie Hazell, CBE

Professor John F. Healy

Professor John Hedgecoe

Derek Heys, CBE, TD

Sir Tom Hickinbotham, KCMG, KCVO, CIE, OBE

Sir William Hildred, CB, OBE

Lord Hill of Luton

Professor Colin B. Hindley

Professor Charles R. Hiscocks

Brian H. Holbeche, CBE

Colonel Sir Tom Hood, KBE, CB, TD, DL

Major-General Gerald C. Hopkinson, CB, DSO, OBE, MC

Professor Robert J. Hopper

Sir Walter S. Howard, MBE, DL

The Rt. Hon. Denis Howell, MP

Vice-Admiral Sir Charles Hughes Hallett, KCB, CBE

John L. Hunt, MP

Colonel Geoffrey T. Hurrell, OBE

Sir John Inch, CVO, CBE, QPM

Professor John D. Ivins

Hector B. Jacks

Gordon Jacob, CBE

The Hon. Greville Janner, QC, MP

Sir William Jenkin, CSI, CIE, KPM

Percival H. Jennings, CBE

Sir Maynard Jenour, TD, JP

Brigadier Robert Jephson-Jones, GC

Captain James H. Jobling

Sir Glyn Jones, GCMG, MBE

Alexander J. Kellar, CMG, OBE

David Kelly

Sir Peter Kent, FRS

Judge James Kingham

Rear-Admiral M.D. Kyrle Pope, CB, MBE

Major-General Stanley E. Large, MBE, MD, FRCP

Major-General Arundell R. Leakey, CB, DSO, MC

Air Chief Marshal Sir Peter Le Cheminant, GBE, KCB, DFC

Major-General Richard E. Lloyd, CB, CBE, DSO

Judge David Lloyd-Jones, VRD

Sir Norman Longley, CBE, DL

Air Commodore John C. Macdonald, CB, CBE, DFC, AFC

Brigadier Archibald G. Mackenzie-Kennedy, CBE, DSO

Air Vice-Marshal Donald F. MacLeod, CB

Lord McNair
Professor William S. Maguinness
Sir Frank Marshall
The Late Sir Arthur Massey, CBE
The Earl of Mexborough
The Rev. Lord Milverton
Professor Ross G. Mitchell
Kenneth More, CBE
Professor H. Gemmell Morgan
Lieut.-General Thomas L. Morony, OBE
The Rt. Hon. Charles Morris, MP
Alexander S. Mountfield
Professor Kenneth Muir
The Rt. Hon. Len Murray, OBE

Sir Basil Nield, CBE, DL
Rear-Admiral Harry D. Nixon, CB, MVO, DL
Sir Arthur Norrington, JP

Professor John Osborne

Lieut.-Colonel Sir Julian Paget, Bt
Victor G. Paige, CBE
Lord Parry
Sir John Paul, GCMG, OBE, MC
Brigadier Sir Otho Prior-Palmer, DSO
Magnus Pyke, OBE

Sir Stanley Rous, CBE, JP

Mike Sammes
Barry Granger Smallman, CMG, CVO

S. Taylor
Sir Herbert Todd, CIE

Lord Willis

INDEX

Figures in parentheses indicate the number of stories on the same subject and page.

234

A WORD FROM OXFAM

Buying this book is one of many ways of helping OXFAM's work. You might also like to support your local OXFAM shop, by buying cards, handicrafts from overseas, or by taking along articles for them to sell.

You can also help us in a very direct and simple way by filling in one of the forms below. You may make a single payment, or regular payments. If you decide to pay regularly for four years, send back the Tax Recovery Form with your Banker's Order.

We will be able to claim an extra 50p from the tax man for every £1 you give. That way, your help for the needy overseas goes 50% further.

Simply fill in the forms below, cut out and return them to: OXFAM, 274 Banbury Road, Oxford OX2 7DZ.

USE THIS FORM TO GIVE ONCE TO OXFAM

I enclose cheque for £ _____ payable to OXFAM.

FULL NAME (in capitals) _____

ADDRESS _____

PTPA1

USE THIS FORM TO GIVE REGULARLY TO OXFAM

BANKER'S ORDER FORM

To the Manager _____ (Name of Bank)

at _____ (Bank Address)

_____

Please pay OXFAM £ _____ **every**

month/year starting on _____ **(date) until further notice.**

Name _____

Address _____

_____

_____

Signed _____

FOR OFFICE USE
To Barclays Bank, High Street, Oxford (20 65 31) A/c 60646792/60646784 quoting our reference. _____

PTPA1

USE THIS FORM TO MAKE YOUR GIFT GO TWICE AS FAR

TAX RECOVERY FORM

I, _____ FULL NAME (in capitals)

of _____ (Address)

_____

Date _____ Signed _____

(To complete this form, get a friend to witness your signature)
Witness's Signature _____

Witness's Address _____

_____

undertake to pay OXFAM each year for four years (or during my lifetime, if shorter) from today the sum that will, after the deduction of income tax at the basic rate be

£ _____ *

(LS)

* Just put here the amount you wish to pay annually and we do the rest.

PTPA1